OXFORD Business English

BUSINESS FOCUS

PRE-INTERMEDIATE WORKBOOK

C0-CEC-099

David Grant

Robert McLarty

UNIVERSITY PRESS

OXFORD
UNIVERSITY PRESS

Great Clarendon Street, Oxford OX2 6DP

Oxford University Press is a department of the University of Oxford.
It furthers the University's objective of excellence in research, scholarship,
and education by publishing worldwide in

Oxford New York

Auckland Cape Town Dar es Salaam Hong Kong Karachi
Kuala Lumpur Madrid Melbourne Mexico City Nairobi
New Delhi Shanghai Taipei Toronto

With offices in

Argentina Austria Brazil Chile Czech Republic France Greece
Guatemala Hungary Italy Japan Poland Portugal Singapore
South Korea Switzerland Thailand Turkey Ukraine Vietnam

OXFORD and OXFORD ENGLISH are registered trade marks of
Oxford University Press in the UK and in certain other countries

© Oxford University Press 2004

The moral rights of the author have been asserted

Database right Oxford University Press (maker)

First published 2004

2009 2008 2007 2006 2005
10 9 8 7 6 5 4 3 2

ISBN-13: 978-0-19-437976-2
ISBN-10: 0-19-437976-0

Printed in China

ACKNOWLEDGEMENTS

*The authors and publisher are grateful to those who have given
permission to reproduce the following extracts and adaptations of
copyright material:*

p13 Extract from www.screenblock.com/inventor.htm.
Reproduced by permission.

p23 Extract from 'I'm always adding strings to my bow' by
Bryony Gordon, The Daily Telegraph, 11 June 2002. ©
Telegraph Group Limited 2002. Reproduced by permission.

p29 Extract from 'Trusting the customer' from
www.thewowawards.com/winners/ritchie.htm. Supplied
with permission of Derek Williams, the WOW! Awards
www.TheWowAwards.com

p25 Extract from 'Farmer forges ahead with a career in iron'
by Maisha Frost, Daily Express, 13 May 2002. Reproduced by
permission of The Express.

p35 Extract from 'Customer Service: The Good, the Bad and
the Ugly' by Keith Regan, E-Commerce Times, July 17, 2000.
Reproduced by permission of Richard Kern, ECT News
Network, Inc.

p59 From 'Don't sweat the small stuff at work' by Richard
Carlson. Copyright © 1999 Richard Carlson. Reprinted by
permission of Hyperion.

Sources
p4 www.bestfoods.com/about
p5, 64 www.fortune.com Best Companies For Women
p12 www.gillette.com/company/historicaltimeline.asp
p30 stephen.brough@profilebooks.co.uk
p41 www.dassault-aviation.com
p42 www.grohe.com
p43 www.boeing.com/employment/melanie
p44-45 www.wrigley.com/wrigley/about/about_story.asp
p57 www.adassoc.org.uk/press/press70
p61 www.fastcompany.com/online

Although every effort has been made to trace and contact
copyright holders before publication, this has not been
possible in some cases. We apologize for any apparent
infringement of copyright and if notified, the publisher will
be pleased to rectify any errors or omissions at the earliest
opportunity.

Acknowledgements
Illustrations by Kate Charlesworth pp 8, 17, 20, 54, 60, 61;
Bob Dewar pp 14, 23, 31, 37, 46, 59; Rose Hardy p 52
Commissioned photography by MM Studios pp 4, 35, 44

*We would also like to thank the following for permission to reproduce
the following photographs:* Action Plus p 48 (G.Kirk); Alamy pp
5, 19 (F.Chmura), 51 (A.Parada/turkey), (D.Hurst/lemon),
(Foodfolio/strawberry), (Comstock Images/sake);
Anthony Blake Photo Library pp 51 (P.de Villiers/mineral
water), (R.Clark/onion); Courtesy of Philippe Chemel p 24;
Corbis royalty free p 24 (glider); Courtesy of Dassault
Aviation p 41; Getty Images pp 10 (C.Fortuna), 26
(R.Lockyer), 56 (Digital Vision), 62 (G.Pease); © 2003 The
Gillette Company p 12; By kind permission of Grohe Water
Technology AG &Co KG p 42; Courtesy of P & O Nedlloyd
p 6; Courtesy of www.screenblock.com p 13; Reproduced
with permission of Derek Williams, The WOW! Awards –
www.TheWowAwards.com p 29

Contents

1 Making contact 4

2 Sharing information 10

3 Visiting companies 16

4 Making decisions 22

5 Comparing information 28

6 Dealing with problems 34

7 Presenting information 40

8 Entertaining 46

9 Taking part in meetings 52

10 Managing your time 58

Tapescript 64

Answer key 69

FOCUS ON WORDS: *Company facts and activities*

1   Complete the questions with these words.

What	Where	Who	Do	How many	What	Who	Does

1   .... do you work for?
2   .... does the company do?
3   .... are you based?
4   .... employees are there?
5   .... the company pay well?
6   .... is your annual turnover?
7   .... are your main competitors?
8   .... you have any well-known brands?

2   Read the company profile below and complete the gaps with these words.

competition	production facilities	brands	head office	CEO
products	advertising	sales	company	employees

Bestfoods is an American food [1]... with its

[2]................................. in New Jersey. Its most famous [3]...................................

include Knorr soups, Hellman's mayonnaise and Skippy peanut butter. The company

has [4]................................. in sixty countries and sells its [5]................................. in

about 110. It has 44,000 [6]................................. and [7]................................. of

about $9 billion. Charles R Shoemate is the [8]................................. . In the food

industry there is a lot of [9]................................. and Bestfoods spends a lot of

money on [10]................................. to retain its market share.

(((1.1)))   **3**   *Competition* has four syllables: *com•pe•ti•tion*. The third syllable is stressed. Look at these pairs of words. Tick (✓) the one that has the stressed syllable underlined correctly. Then listen, check and repeat.

1   compet<u>i</u>tion   .....✔....   <u>com</u>petition   ....✗.....
2   <u>com</u>petitor   ....   compet<u>i</u>tor   ....✓.....
3   indust<u>ry</u>   ....   <u>in</u>dustry   ....✓.....
4   manuf<u>ac</u>ture   ....✓....   <u>man</u>ufacture   ....
5   fact<u>o</u>ry   ....   <u>fac</u>tory   ....✓.....
6   employ<u>ee</u>   ....✓....   <u>em</u>ployee   ....
7   person<u>nel</u>   ....   <u>per</u>sonnel   ....
8   ad<u>ver</u>tising   ....   <u>ad</u>vertising   ....

Listen to this profile of an American company and answer the questions below.

1 Where is the company based?
- ❏ a Washington.
- ❏ b Wisconsin.
- ❏ c West Virginia.

2 What does it do?
- ❏ a It publishes books.
- ❏ b It runs hotels.
- ❏ c It sells clothing.

3 Does it employ mainly women?
- ❏ a Yes, it does.
- ❏ b Not sure.
- ❏ c No, it doesn't.

4 Why is it a good company to work for?
- ❏ a It pays well and offers good training.
- ❏ b It offers free clothing.
- ❏ c There are 100 new jobs every year.

5 Are there many competitors?
- ❏ a Not sure.
- ❏ b Yes, there are.
- ❏ c No, there aren't.

Listen to the text again and complete these sentences.

1 Lands' End, Inc. is a clothing company .... in Dodgeville, Wisconsin.
2 It is a mail-order company selling its .... through catalogues and the Internet.
3 It has twenty-three .... in the US employing 4,150 people.
4 It .... another thousand staff abroad.
5 Over three quarters of the .... are female.
6 The company offers an average of 60 hours' .... per person annually.
7 With a starting .... of over $21,000 for .... staff and over $40,000 for professional people, it is a popular place to work.
8 In 2001 it had over 10,000 .... for just over one hundred new jobs!
9 .... in 2001 was $1,320 m.
10 In a market with so much ...., Lands' End, Inc. is doing very well.

▶▶▶▶▶ **FOCUS EXTRA**: *Saying large numbers*

1

Complete the table with these numbers and then write out the numbers in full, as in the example.

1876	543,955	49,000,000	58,000,000,000
1,502	979	17,210,800	66,000,000

	FIGURES	WORDS
1 Transfer fee of Zinedine Zidane from Juventus to Real Madrid (pounds)	49,000,000	*Forty-nine million*
2 Boeing's turnover in 2001 (dollars)		
3 Population of Australia		
4 Annual number of passengers at Chicago Airport		
5 The year the telephone was invented		
6 Number of passengers who died on the Titanic		
7 The height of Angel Falls in Venezuela (metres)		
8 The area of France (square kilometres)		

Listen and check your answers. Then listen again and repeat.

FOCUS ON GRAMMAR: *Present simple and present continuous*

1 Read the profile and complete the gaps with these verbs in the correct present simple form.

be	contain	fly	have	live	play
go	spend	take	transport	travel	work

Roger McLarty ¹ *is* a ship's captain. He ² for P&O Nedlloyd, which is an Anglo-Dutch company. His ship always ³ the same route from the west coast of the USA to the Far East. Roger ⁴ three months on board and then ⁵ three months' holiday. At the start of a trip he ⁶ from England, where he ⁷ , to join the ship at some point on the route. The ship ⁸ containers from port to port. The boxes ⁹ everything under the sun from cereals to electronic goods, from machine tools to pharmaceutical products. During a voyage he doesn't ¹⁰ a lot of spare time because there is a tight schedule to meet. When he is on leave he ¹¹ golf or he ¹² skiing.

2 Look at the text again and make questions for these answers, as in the example.

1 *What is his job* ?
   He's a ship's captain.
2 *Who* ?
   He works for P&O Nedlloyd.
3 *How long* ?
   He spends three months on board.
4 *Where* ?
   It travels between the USA and the Far East.
5 *What* ?
   It transports containers.
6 *Why* ?
   Because the schedule is very tight.
7 *What* ?
   He plays golf and skis.

3 Match the questions 1–6 to the answers a–f, as in the example.

1 Who's calling?   a With friends.
2 What car do you drive? b A Peugeot 207.
3 Where are you staying? c They're waiting for Tomas.
4 Do you travel a lot?   d My name is Nils Hatt.
5 Is the Financial Director there? e No, I don't.
6 What are Dik and Heinrich doing? f Yes, she is.

4 Find the mistake in each of these sentences and correct it, as in the example.

1 What you doing?
   ...*What are you doing?*...

2 He works in Turin but he live in Milan.

   ....

3 What sort of books you like?

   ....

4 I'm speaking Spanish and a little French.

   ....

5 She loves white wine but she don't like red at all.

   ....

6 Where he works?

   ....

5 Complete these dialogues by putting the verbs in brackets into the correct form (present simple or continuous).

A What (Jack / do) [1] .... right now?
B He (speak) [2] .... to a new customer.
A What about you?
B I (prepare) [3] .... next year's budget.
A Can you help me with my computer?
B Sure.

C Who (you / work) [4] .... for?
D At the moment I (work) [5] .... as a temp in London but I (look)
   [6] .... for something permanent. What about you?
C I (work) [7] .... for Novo Nordisk. It's a Danish pharmaceutical
   company.
D What (you / do) [8] ....?
C I work in Research and Development.

E Hi, Mary, it's Emily.
F Where (you / call) [9] .... from?
E I'm in Rome on a language course. I (learn) [10] .... Italian.
F Where (you / stay) [11] ....?
E I (live) [12] .... with an Italian family for four weeks. They're great.
F Lucky you!

1   Look at the cartoons above and write requests, using *Can / Could I* or *Can / Could you* and these words.

borrow	ask	give	have
use	send	the Internet	me a hand
me a brochure	your magazine	a question	another drink

2   Complete the dialogues with these expressions.

I'm afraid not	I'm afraid	Certainly
Of course	Sorry about that	No problem

A   Can I borrow some money for lunch?
B   ¹ _____ you can. How much do you need?
A   Can you spare five pounds?
B   Yes, sure. ² _____. Here you are.

C   Could you come in on Saturday? Paolo is sick.
D   Oh dear. ³ _____ I'm busy on Saturday.
    ⁴ _____.
C   That's OK. Maybe Laura can come.

E   Could I make a quick call, please?
F   ⁵ _____. Where are you calling?
E   Tokyo. Is that OK?
F   Well, no, ⁶ _____. You can only make national calls from this phone.

3 Complete the dialogue with these words, as in the example.

urgent	number	afraid	message	call	calling
mobile	line	speak	through	~~speaking~~	help

A Hello, Ballpark Chemicals, Caroline [1] _speaking_ . How can I help?

B This is Dr James Mackay. I'm [2] _____ from Robertson's in Edinburgh. Could I [3] _____ to Joanna Stewart, please?

A I'm [4] _____ Joanna is away today. Can I put you [5] _____ to her assistant?

B Thank you.

A Hold the [6] _____ a second.

C Hello, R&D, Dick Rogers speaking.

B Hello, Dick, this is James Mackay. I understand Joanna is away.

C Yes, she's at a conference in Milan. Can I [7] _____?

B Could I leave a [8] _____?

C Sure.

B Could you ask her to [9] _____ me. It's quite [10] _____.

C Has she got your [11] _____?

B I think so, but take my [12] _____ number: 0773569412.

C OK, I'll tell her.

B Thanks very much for your help.

C Nice talking to you, James. Bye now.

B Goodbye.

END-OF-UNIT PUZZLE Find thirteen words, with three letters or more, from the Student's Book unit in the grid below, as in the examples. You can read the words horizontally (left to right) or vertically (top to bottom).

```
H W M B H O L H G B X P Q
C O M P E T I T O R X R E
O B A Z A C T B U Y G O H
M K R C D O E B R A N D B
P I K O Q P L Z S T I U U
A X E N U M Q Z V T E C S
N Y T S A R E C R U I T I
Y S T U R N O V E R G F N
D A Z M T A C E G I K M E
T L B E E M P L O Y E E S
L E B R R A C V N C Y O S
Z S O T S R E T A I L E R
O P E R A T E X U F A N V
```

..._competitor_.... ....

..._headquarters_.. ....

....

FOCUS ON WORDS: *Development of products and services*

1   A product manager is talking about her work. Complete the missing verbs, as in the example. The first two letters are given.

A   What does your job involve exactly?

B   I am involved at all stages of the process from the moment we
    1 *design* a new product to the moment we 2 *la* .... it and start to 3 *se* .... it.

A   What does the R & D team do?

B   With any new product they do tests to 4 *im* .... the quality of the product or the manufacturing processes. With a shampoo, for example, they might 5 *de* .... a new formula which is easier to make or cheaper to 6 *pr* ....

A   Do you work with the marketing team as well?

B   Yes. When we have a new product the marketing team ask customers to 7 *tr* .... it to give us feedback. Often with a new product we 8 *ad* .... in the press and on radio, and they organize all that.

2   Complete the word families in this table, as in the example.

NOUN	VERB
product	produce
sale	1
concept	conceive
2	develop
design	3
4	promote
launch	5
advertising	6
improvement	7
8	trial

3   Now complete these sentences with words from the table, as in the example.

1   In 2002 I became a *Product* .... Manager at JK Foods.
2   Next year we are going to .... a new engine in our Slovakian factory.
3   We did a product .... with over two thousand customers.
4   The original .... came from the Managing Director's grandson.
5   The design team made a big .... to the shape of the bottle.
6   .... should be high in Western Europe.
7   We are planning to .... the product on the market in June.
8   We allocated over €200,000 for TV .... last year.

4 Some of the words in **2** are often used with other words. Complete these sentences with words from the box.

| design | launch | sales | trials |
| improved | development | advertising | product |

1 January 8th is the .... *date* for the software products.
2 We are planning a huge .... *campaign*.
3 Our food scientists are working on a very interesting .... *project* at the moment.
4 A new, ... *version* of our salad cream is coming out next month.
5 We did a lot of *consumer* .... to get the flavour right.
6 We used *computer-assisted* .... on the new label.
7 We have now got a very wide .... *range*.
8 .... *forecasts* for next year look good.

5 Match each word in A to a word in B which has a similar meaning.

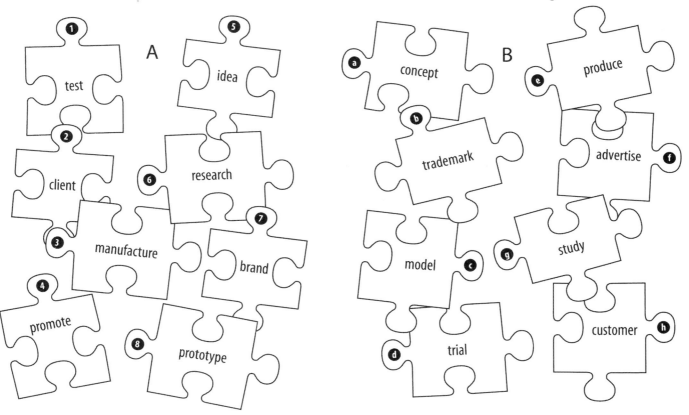

(((2.1))) **6** All the words in *italics* below have two syllables. Which one is stressed? Underline the stressed syllable, as in the example. Listen and check. Then listen again and repeat.

1 We are very pleased with this new *product*.
2 We now want to *improve* the rest of the range.
3 Our factory can *produce* 800 units per day.
4 I work for a *service* company.
5 We are trying to increase our *market* share.
6 Our *design* team won an award last year.
7 It is important to *research* the competition before launching a new product.
8 The advertising *campaign* lasted two months.

FOCUS ON GRAMMAR: *Past simple*

1 Read this article about the American multinational Gillette and put the verbs in brackets into the past simple form, as in the example.

Very occasionally a man has an idea which changes the lives of millions. King Camp Gillette (have) [1] *had* one in 1895 when he (conceive) [2] .... the idea of the safety razor. Before that, men (go) [3] .... to the barber's for a shave or (take) [4] .... a long time using a cut-throat razor. In 1901 Gillette (found) [5] .... his company in Boston and sales (grow)

[6] .... so fast that in 1905 he (open) [7] .... his first office in Europe, in London. Gillette (be) [8] .... a skilful advertiser and today the company continues to spend huge sums of money advertising in the press and on TV, or sponsoring major sports events. In 1950 Gillette (pay) [9] .... $6,000,000 to sponsor the baseball World Series for

six years. Back in 1908 the company (design) [10] .... its famous diamond-shaped logo. Just a few years later, in 1917, Gillette (win) [11] .... one of its largest contracts ever. It (supply) [12] .... the US army with razors during the First World War. In 1930, in order to gain market share, it (merge) [13] .... with a competitor, Gaisman's Razor Company, and from there went from strength to strength. After the resignation of King Camp Gillette in 1931, the company (continue) [14] .... to diversify and in 1936 it (launch) [15] .... brushless shaving cream, which is still one of Gillette's most important products.

2 Read the article again and answer these questions.
1 When did Gillette have the idea for the safety razor? ....
2 How did men shave before the safety razor? ....
3 What shape was the Gillette logo? ....
4 Who bought a lot of razors in 1917? ....
5 What product did the company launch in 1936? ....
6 What event did it sponsor in the fifties? ....

3 Now make questions for these answers, as in the example.
1 *When did King Camp Gillette found his company* ....?
   He founded it in 1901.
2 *Where* ....?
   He opened it in London.
3 *How much* ....?
   $6,000,000.
4 *When* ....?
   In 1908.
5 *What* ....?
   A US army contract.
6 *Why* ....?
   To gain market share.

4 Read this article and decide if the statements below are true (T) or false (F).

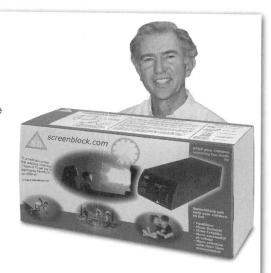

I am the inventor of Screenblock, a device which I designed to stop children watching too much television. I can't say that I had a carefully conceived business plan for my device – I invented it because I was a desperate man! I noticed that my two children aged 9 and 11 watched too much TV when they were not at school and we had huge arguments if I tried to switch it off. I had the idea that it would be better if the TV switched off automatically rather than when a parent pressed the button.

It is a very simple design. It stops power flowing from the electricity supply to the TV at pre-set times. In this way you can limit the number of hours children watch for. It is a rectangular box about 20 cm long. You lift the lid on the box, plug the TV in, close the lid and lock it. You then plug the Screenblock in.

I had two prototypes before we found the perfect design. I tested the product a lot at home and with friends and little by little we developed Screenblock as it is today. Towards the end of 2001 we decided to launch it. I costed the device at just under $150, which is not too expensive. We advertised on the Internet and I created a website to explain the product. I also did some interviews on the radio and in newspapers and we soon started to take orders. Users talked to friends and the word soon spread.

1 Tony had a carefully conceived business plan. ....
2 The Screenblock stops the supply of electricity to the TV. ....
3 It is rectangular. ....
4 Today Screenblock is the same as the original design. ....
5 He tested the product a lot before launching it. ....
6 He didn't advertise. ....
7 He designed a website to describe his device. ....

5 There are fifteen regular verbs in the past simple form in the text above. Make a list.
...*designed*..
....
....

6 Now write an example sentence for five of the verbs, using your own ideas.
....
....
....
....
....

FOCUS ON EXPRESSIONS: *Starting a conversation and keeping a conversation going*

1 Complete the three dialogues below with these expressions.

Pleased to meet you, Roger.	Let me introduce you to some people.
Let me introduce you to Sally Dutton.	Nice to meet you, too.
Is this your first day?	Do you know many people here?
Have we met before?	Are you new?

A Excuse me?

B Yes?

A ¹ ....

B I don't think so.

A ² ....

B Yes, I am. I started yesterday. My name's Jenny Porter.

A Nice to meet you, Jenny. I'm Beatrice. Beatrice Kahn.

C Jack?

D Yes?

C ³ .... Sally, this is Jack.

D Nice to meet you.

E ⁴ ....

D ⁵ ....

E No, I don't. I'm quite new.

F Good morning.

G Good morning.

F ⁶ ....

G Yes, it is.

F Right. ⁷ .... What's your name?

G Hall. Roger Hall.

F ⁸ .... Let me introduce you to the receptionists.

14

2 Complete the gaps in these questions with the words from the box.

much	far	long	many	high	often

1 How .... children have you got?
2 How .... do you speak English at work?
3 How .... time have you got?
4 How .... is this session?
5 How .... is that building?
6 How .... is the hotel? I'm really tired.

3 Now match the questions in **2** to these answers.

a About 200 metres. Impressive, isn't it? ....
b Thirty minutes – it finishes at 11.00. ....
c Every day at the moment. ....
d Three, all girls. ....
e About ten kilometres. Do you want to leave? ....
f About ten minutes, then I have another appointment. ....

4 Complete the follow-up questions in these mini-dialogues, using the words in brackets.

1 A I like going to the cinema and I'm interested in reading.
  B Oh really? .... (kind of books / like)
2 A I went on holiday to Australia last year.
  B Did you? .... (places / visit)
3 A I'm a doctor in a company medical centre.
  B Are you? .... (hours / work)
4 A I love Indian food.
  B Me too. .... (favourite dish / be)
5 A My company has 10,000 employees.
  B Wow! .... (countries / operate in)

(((2.2))) **END-OF-UNIT PUZZLE**

SMALL TALK QUIZ

What do we say in these situations?

1 Listen and choose the best answer, a, b, or c.

2 Now listen to the complete dialogues and check your answers.

	a	b	c
1	☐ No, I don't.	☐ Yes, we have.	☐ Really.
2	☐ Me too.	☐ No, I can't.	☐ Yes, I am.
3	☐ Really?	☐ Nor me.	☐ No, it isn't.
4	☐ And you.	☐ Great!	☐ Me too.
5	☐ Who?	☐ Is it?	☐ Nice to meet you.
6	☐ Fine, and you?	☐ Worse.	☐ Perfect.
7	☐ No, I don't.	☐ Yes, we have.	☐ Yes, from time to time.
8	☐ How do you do?	☐ Well, and you?	☐ Do what?

FOCUS ON WORDS: *Company visits and travel*

1   A is visiting C's company to present his products. B is the receptionist. Complete these extracts from the conversation with the words from the box.

do	attend	look	have	sign
meet	pass	give	negotiate	

A   Good morning. I ¹ .... an appointment with Mrs Forster.

B   Certainly, sir. Would you like to ² .... in, and I'll tell Mrs Forster you're here.

A   Yes, sure.

B   Here's your security ³ .... You'll need to show it when you go through that door.

C   So would you like a ⁴ .... round the company before you ⁵ .... your presentation?

A   No, thanks. But I have one or two questions. Do you know how many people are going to ⁶ .... ?

A   So now you've seen our products, do you think you can ⁷ .... business with us?

C   Yes, definitely. Perhaps we can ⁸ .... again next week to ⁹ .... conditions of the contract.

2   Read the text below and decide if the statements on the next page are true (T) or false (F).

Zurich's Hotel for Women Only

Business travel can be difficult for everyone, but especially for women. Travelling alone in a strange city, women often don't want to go out at night and visit local attractions themselves. Dining alone at a restaurant can be depressing. Many women spend the evening in their hotel rooms – using room service, watching television and eating snacks from the mini-bar. Life is not always so exciting for a travelling businesswoman.

That's why a new hotel in Zurich, Switzerland, offers an interesting alternative for women business travellers – a 'women-only' hotel. The Lady's First Hotel and Wellness Center opened in January, 2001. Men aren't allowed in, and all the staff are female.

The hotel was designed by architect Pia Schmid, with women business travellers in mind. It is a small hotel with 28 rooms. Guests can meet in the lounge in the lobby, and sit around a fireplace. Light refreshments are available in the hotel bar and mini-bar snacks include healthy food, not only chocolate and alcohol. Bathrooms are well-lit and have extra amenities. Meeting and conference rooms are available.

The best aspect of Lady's First is the Wellness Center. The facilities are located on the top floor of the hotel and offer a wide variety of health and beauty treatments including massages and jet-lag treatments. The Wellness Center has a steam room, saunas and a terrace overlooking the lake and mountains.

1 Women travelling alone often prefer to stay in their hotel rooms. ....
2 The hotel only employs women. ....
3 There isn't any chocolate or alcohol in the mini-bar. ....
4 There aren't any meeting rooms. ....
5 The Wellness Center is near reception. ....
6 You have a beautiful view from the Wellness Center. ....

3 Now find words and expressions in the text that correspond to these definitions. The first letter of each word is given.

1 places of tourist interest: *l*................ *a*................
2 eating in a restaurant: *d*................
3 you eat these between meals: *s*................ or *l*................ *r*................
4 a room where you can sit and relax: *l*................
5 an open space inside a hotel near reception: *l*................
6 good for your physical condition: *h*................
7 having good lights: *w*................ - *l*................
8 things to make life easier / more pleasant: *a*................ or *f*................

4 Where can you hear the sentences below? Match them to pictures a–d, as in the example. There are two sentences for each picture.

1 One-way or return? ...*c*......
2 Do you have one to rent for today? ....
3 I'm looking for Gate 45. ....
4 Can I check out, please? ....
5 Is this the platform for Munich? ....
6 Is there a petrol station near here? ....
7 Do you have any bags to check in? ....
8 Single or double? ....

5 Now match 1–8 in 4 to these responses, as in the example.

a I'm not sure. There's a timetable over there if you want to check. ...5....
b It's just for me. Is there a safe in the room? ....
c If you're going south, there's one about 30 km down the motorway. ....
d No, I don't. Can you tell me what time we're boarding? ....
e Yes. That'll be €74, including insurance. ....
f I'm not sure. Is the fare cheaper if I pay for both journeys now? ....
g You're in the wrong part of the terminal. It's over there on the left. ....
h Sure. I'll just prepare your bill. ....

FOCUS ON GRAMMAR: *Countable and uncountable nouns*

1 Mark these words countable (C) or uncountable (U), as in the examples.

car	..C....	money	..U....	office	....	luggage	....
room	....	phone	....	cash	....	shop	....
news	....	information	....	space	....	desk	....
traffic	....	bag	....	help	....	bank	....

2 You are at an airport and you want some information. Complete your questions with these words. You can use some words more than once.

a	an	some	any	is	are	much	many

1 I want to rent .... car. .... there a car rental office here?

2 I'd like to leave my luggage here for the day. How .... does it cost?

3 .... there .... phones here which accept phone cards?

4 How .... days a week is the bank open?

5 I want to change .... money. Are there .... currency exchange desks here?

6 I see that you have .... rooms to rent for meetings. How .... space do they have?

7 I don't have .... information about tourist attractions in Warsaw. Is there .... information desk in the airport?

8 I need .... cash, but there .... not a cash machine here in Departures. Is there one in the Arrival area?

9 I want to send .... postcards but I don't have .... stamps. Where can I buy them?

10 There .... not .... duty-free shops here. Am I in the wrong place?

3 Now look at the information about Warsaw Airport on the next page and answer the questions in **2**, as in the example.

1 Yes, ..there is............... . In fact, ..there are six in the Arrival area................................... .

2 Certainly. It ....

3 Yes, ... In fact, most ....

4 It's open .... a week, but .... early on Saturdays.

5 Yes, ... In fact, there ....

6 I'm not sure, but if you want more information, ...

7 Yes, ... There's a ....

8 Yes, ... In fact, there ....

9 There's ....

10 Yes, you are. All the duty-free shops ....

Facilities at Warsaw's Frederic Chopin Airport

Car rental:	Six in Arrival area, lower level
Post Office:	Departure area, open Monday to Friday 8.00–20.00
Phones:	All over the airport, most take phone cards
Cash machines:	Two in Arrival area by the newspaper kiosk
Shopping:	Newspaper stands, florist, jewellery store. Duty-free shops after passport control
Left luggage:	Arrival area, open 24 hours; cost – 24 zl
Banks:	Powszechny Bank Kredytowy S.A. has a branch in the Arrival area, open 7.30–18.00 Monday to Friday, 7.30–13.00 on Saturdays
Currency exchange:	Nine desks in both Arrival and Departure areas
Meeting facilities:	Conference space available for rental; enquire at information desk
Tourist Information Centre:	In Arrival area, open Monday to Sunday 8.00–19.00

(((3.1))) **4** Listen to a passenger talking to three different people at Warsaw Airport. Look again at the list of facilities above, and decide where she is in each conversation.

1 ....   3 ....

2 ....

▶▶▶▶▶ **FOCUS EXTRA:** *Times*

Read about Tom's typical working day. Decide what time it is at each stage of his day and complete the gaps with one of these times, as in the example. You will not need all the times.

four fifty	quarter to two	twenty past eight	twenty-five to ten
eight thirty-five	one thirty	twenty to eleven	four forty-five
five thirty	~~eight o'clock~~	quarter past eleven	five to seven
five past eight	half past twelve	four fifteen	ten past ten

Yesterday Tom got up at seven thirty. Half an hour later (¹ *eight o'clock* ....) he left home and drove to work. The journey usually takes half an hour, but there wasn't much traffic, so he arrived ten minutes early (² ....). He spent quarter of an hour looking at his email (³ ....). Then he had a 'one-hour' meeting, which finished thirty-five minutes late (⁴ ....). After this he made a half-hour phone call (⁵ ....). Before lunch he had a meeting with a client. This lasted a bit less than two hours (⁶ ....). He usually takes one hour for lunch, but the restaurant service was slow, and he got back to work a quarter of an hour late (⁷ ....). He then had a long two and a half hour meeting (⁸ ....). After this he spent half an hour on the phone (⁹ ....), and three-quarters of an hour talking with his boss (¹⁰ ....). Before going home, he had a report to finish. This took him just under an hour and a half (¹¹ ....).

FOCUS ON EXPRESSIONS: *Making offers and greeting visitors*

1   Look at the dialogue below. An auditor (B) is visiting A's company. A is a little nervous. Complete A's offers with one of these words or expressions. You can use some expressions more than once.

Shall   Would you like a   Would you like to   Would you like me to

A   Please take a seat.

B   Thanks very much.

A   ¹... coffee?

B   No, thanks, I'm fine. It's a little hot in here.

A   Yes, it is. ²... switch on the air-conditioning?

B   Yes, please, if you could.

A   OK. That should be better now. ³... meet the CEO before we start?

B   Well, I'd like to speak to him before I leave. But it's really the Chief Accountant I need to see first.

A   ⁴... I ask him to come in now?

B   Can I just have five minutes to get my papers ready?

A   Yes, sure.

B   Er, I don't seem to have your most recent bank statements.

A   Oh dear. ⁵... I go and find them?

B   Yes, please. I do have to look at all your official financial documents.

A   Yes of course. ⁶... see the statements just for the last three months?

B   No, I think the last twelve months would be better.

A   OK. I'll make some copies for you.

2   Match sentences 1–7 with responses a–g, as in the example.

1   I really love your new product range.

2   I'm afraid I can't come this evening.

3   I'd like to invite you for dinner.

4   Shall I open the door for you?

5   Thank you for seeing me today.

6   Would you like another drink?

7   I'm sorry it's so noisy in here.

a   That's a pity. Some other time maybe.

b   It's a pleasure.

c   I'm pleased to hear that.

d   Yes, please. The same again.

e   Don't worry. My office is the same.

f   That would be nice.

g   No, that's OK, thanks. I can manage.

3 An Argentinian businessman is meeting a customer at Buenos Aires Airport. Put the conversation in the correct order 1–12. The first is done for you.

☐ Yes, thanks. But I'm a little tired.

☐ Yes, it's really beautiful. How long are you here for?

☐ OK, let's find somewhere ... So is this your first trip to Buenos Aires?

☐ Well, if you'd like to see Buenos Aires by night, I'd be very happy to show it to you.

☐ Just three days.

☐ Well, a quick coffee would be nice.

☐ That's very kind of you. I'd like that.

☐ Yes, it is. I've heard it's a very beautiful city.

☐ So you probably won't have much time to visit the city.

☐ I'm not surprised – it was a very long flight. Would you like something to drink here in the airport first?

☐ No, unfortunately not. But I hope to have one evening free, at least.

☐ *1* Welcome to Argentina. Did you have a good trip?

(((3.2))) **4** You are Pat Young. You are visiting a company. Hélène Bayart is welcoming you.

1 Listen to Part One and respond to each sentence. Give a *yes* answer where possible (e.g. when Hélène Bayart offers you a drink).

2 In Part Two you will hear a complete version of the conversation. Listen and compare your responses to the man in the conversation.

END-OF-UNIT PUZZLE

Read the clues below. What is 'this' in each case? To find the answers, combine words from A and B, as in the example.

A

train	fasten	car
shuttle	key	book
shake	check out	have

B

time-table	bus	a look round
hands	a flight	park
of your room	your seatbelt	card

1 This tells you when you can travel by rail. _train timetable_

2 You do this just before your plane takes off. ....

3 You need this to enter your hotel room. ....

4 You can use this to go from the airport to your hotel. ....

5 You do this when you visit a new company. ....

6 This is where you can leave your Mercedes! ....

7 If you don't do this in advance, maybe the plane will be full.

....

8 You do this when you meet a business contact. ....

9 You do this when you leave the hotel. ....

Making decisions
Employment

FOCUS ON WORDS: *Job benefits and recruitment*

1 Regina is thinking of changing jobs. Look at the list of advantages and disadvantages for her present job and complete the missing words. The first letter is given.

Advantages

Five weeks' [1] p................ holiday a year plus public holidays.

A good [2] p............ plan with the possibility to [3] r............ at age 60.

Free language [4] t............ in English.

Good medical [5] i............ for only €15 a month.

Can use company [6] m............ phone for personal calls!

Disadvantages

Working hours not [7] f............ : have to work 9 to 5, five days a week.

Maternity [8] l............ : 6 months on full pay (but boss thinks work and babies don't mix!).

Not very interesting work. Have asked for more responsibility at annual [9] a............ with boss, but he never listens!

Very low monthly [10] s............ compared with other companies.

2 Complete the word families in this table, as in the example.

VERB	NOUN	
insure	[1] *insurance* / [2] *insurer*	
3	adviser	
apply	4	
5	recruiter	
interview	interview / [6]	/ [7]
8	training / [9]	
10	employee / [11]	/ [12]
13	consultation / [14]	

3 Read this text about a modern phenomenon and decide if the sentences below are true (T) or false (F).

The idea of having one job, and that for life, has gone. In its place is the idea shared by over one million people in Britain that you need to have several jobs *simultaneously*. Why has this happened?

The first reason is purely financial. Many people find that with the high cost of living, particularly in terms of rent or buying property, one salary is simply not *enough*. That is why you find teachers, nurses and policemen stocking the shelves in supermarkets at the weekend or during the night.

The second reason is often because a *hobby* becomes as important as the main job and people have to make a decision. Hugh Montgomerie is a bone specialist at one of London's leading hospitals. Ten years ago he started writing, *initially* a story for his godchildren for Christmas. It soon became his first novel. It won an *award* in 2000 and he is now busy at work on his second. He

continues to work at the hospital.

Sacha Taylor-Cox works for a commercial radio station as Head of Press. In her spare time she is in charge of PR for a number of rock bands. She also runs a business organizing yoga holidays abroad. Sacha says, 'In two years' time I may not want to be in the music business. It's good to have a

back-up plan.'

The other reason people choose to do several things at the same time is the feeling that you only have one life and it is very short. Hugh Montgomerie sees this *regularly* in his main job: 'You only get one *chance* in this life. I intend to use that chance the best I can.'

1 Many people in Britain have more than one job. ....
2 Rents in Britain are quite low. ....
3 Hugh Montgomerie has written two novels. ....
4 He has taken up writing full time. ....
5 Sacha Taylor-Cox's main job is PR work. ....
6 She might not stay in the music business. ....

4 Find words in *italics* in the text that correspond to these definitions, as in the example.

1 at the same time ..*simultaneously*.................................
2 an opportunity ....
3 a leisure activity ....
4 at first ....
5 sufficient ....
6 an alternative arrangement ....
7 often ....
8 a prize ....

FOCUS ON GRAMMAR: *Present perfect and past simple*

1 Read this article about Philippe Chemel and answer the questions below in full sentences, as in the example.

 Philippe Chemel is a pilot with Air France. He flies 747s all over the world. He was born in 1955 and from an early age dreamed of becoming a pilot. At the age of 16 he flew for the first time in a glider. Soon he was a qualified glider pilot and then became an instructor to spend more time in the air. He studied maths and physics in order to be ready to take his pilot's licence and he got a job as a steward to help fund his studies. He worked as an instructor at a

flying club near Paris and finally qualified as a pilot in 1988. For the next two years he worked for an executive airline flying film stars, politicians and business leaders all over the world until, in 1991, he got a

job with Air France. He started flying 747s in 1994. He has flown 747s to many different countries and particularly likes Africa and India.

He loves his job but finds it very tiring and stressful. 'Have you ever had a near miss*?' I asked him. 'Yes,' he replied. 'Last month as I drove on the motorway near Versailles a railway sleeper flew off a truck in front of me. I swerved to avoid it but it hit my Alfa Romeo anyway. I wasn't injured, nor was my daughter. The car was in the garage for two weeks and then I got it back. Just a couple of days later I was stopped at some traffic lights in Paris when I smelt petrol. I got out of my car to look and my car caught fire! Flying is a lot safer.'

near miss: a situation when a serious accident very nearly happens

1 What is Philippe's job? *He's a pilot.*...
2 When was he born? ....
3 How long has he been an airline pilot? ....
4 What did he do for two years? ....
5 How long has he flown 747s? ....
6 Has he visited India? ....
7 Has he had a near miss in the air? ....
8 How long was his car in the garage? ....

2 Look at the article again and make questions for these answers, as in the example.

1 *Which company does Philippe work for?*..
  Air France.

2 ....
  At the age of 16.

3 ....
  To help fund his studies.

4 ....
  At a flying club near Paris.

5 ....
  In 1988.

6 ....
  To many different countries.

7 ....
  Since 1991.

8 ....
  Yes, he has – last month.

3 Complete these sentences with *in*, *for*, *since*, or *never*.

1 Anne Codani started working for BNP .... 1989.
2 She worked there .... ten years.
3 She has worked for Dexia .... 1999.
4 She has been married .... 1993.
5 She and her husband lived in Toulouse .... two years.
6 .... the last few years they have lived in Brussels.
7 She has .... visited South America.
8 Her first child was born .... 1998.

4 Look at this table and complete the questions and answers below, as in the examples.

NAME	COMPANY	STUDIES	MARRIED	CONTINENTS VISITED	RESIDENCE
Peter Agel	Siemens (1989)	Engineering 1982–1988	1991	Europe, N. America, Australia	Munich (1994–)
Mayumi Ishida	Mitsubishi (1997)	English 1994–1996		Asia, Europe, S. America	Nagoya (1998–)
Henrik Svensen	Volvo (2000)	Economics 1992–1995	1999	Europe, N. America	Gothenburg (1995–)
Carla Boni	Pirelli (1990)	Business Admin. 2002–	1991–1996	N. America, Asia, Europe, Australia	Turin (1985–)

1 Has Carla visited South America?   *No, she hasn't.* ....
2 *How long has Peter been married?* ....   Since 1991.
3 ....   Since 1998.
4 Have they all visited North America?   ....
5 When did Henrik join Volvo?   ....
6 ....   In 1990.
7 ....   For six years.
8 ....   Since 1985.

5 Read this report about a man who made a major career change, and put the verbs in brackets into the appropriate tense.

Jim Lawrence (run) [1] *runs* .... a firm with a turnover of over €3 million. Yet only fifteen years ago he (own) [2] .... a farm which was struggling to make a profit. For a few years in the 80s he (work) [3] .... as an estate agent to try and earn some extra money. In 1993 Jim was asked to make an iron candlestick. He (spend) [4] .... €50 to get started and soon had a new business. He received lots of orders and decided to convert his farm buildings to workshops.

'I have had no formal training in iron work,' says Jim, 'but I (always like) [5] .... making things.' These days he employs thirty-two people to help him and he has a very successful business. It is a mail-order company and Jim (recently invest) [6] .... a lot of money in IT to maximize efficiency. During the last fifteen years he (win) [7] .... two very important prizes for business, one in 1996 and the other in 2002.

FOCUS ON EXPRESSIONS: *Making suggestions and arrangements*

1 Three colleagues are discussing a recruitment problem. Read the dialogue and choose the correct alternative in *italics*.

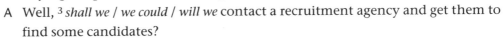

A We've got a lot of orders in the pipeline. I think we need to take on a new person.

B ¹ *Why not / How about / We can* placing an advert on our website? That way, people who are interested in the company will see it.

C I'm not ² *sure / agree / against* about that. Most people who visit the website are interested in buying our products not working for us.

A Well, ³ *shall we / we could / will we* contact a recruitment agency and get them to find some candidates?

B Agencies are usually expensive. ⁴ *What about / If we / We could* put an ad in the local paper. It comes out on Fridays.

C Good ⁵ *thought / opinion / idea*. That way we'll get local people. ⁶ *Maybe I / Shall I / Am I* call them now?

A Yes, ⁷ *fine / well / go*. While you're doing that, why ⁸ *we can't / aren't we / don't we* draft the text?

(((4.1))) **2** Listen to these situations and choose the best suggestion below for each one.

a Why don't you call your doctor and get an appointment? ....

b Why don't we all go away together one weekend and have some fun? ....

c I haven't got much money. Let's just have a sandwich in the canteen. ....

d How about asking for a pay rise? ....

e Let's get the newspapers and see if there are any interesting vacancies. ....

f I think we should advertise it on the website. ....

g Why don't we find another one? How about looking in Yellow Pages? ....

h How about getting a bilingual secretary? ....

3 Today is Wednesday, July 12th. What are the following dates or days?

1	Thursday, July 13th	*tomorrow*
2	....	the day after tomorrow
3	....	last Wednesday
4	Tuesday, July 11th	....
5	....	this Saturday
6	Monday, July 17th	....
7	June	....
8	....	a week today

4 An HR manager has received an interesting CV. She telephones the candidate, Kate Rankin, to arrange an interview. Put the dialogue in the correct order 1–16.

☐ Yes I did. That's why I'm calling. Could you come to Paris one day next week?

☐ We're interviewing on Wednesday and Thursday. Are you available on Wednesday afternoon?

☐ Yes, it's on the CV.

☐ Thanks for calling. Bye.

☐ This is Claire Palies. I'm calling from Sanofi.

☐ I'll send you an email with directions. It's very simple.

☐ Lovely. What time is good for you? Shall we say three o'clock?

1 Hello? Could I speak to Kate Rankin?

☐ Yes, I think so. What day did you have in mind?

☐ Yes, of course it is. OK then, I'll see you next Wednesday.

☐ Oh hello. You got my CV, then?

☐ Wait a second. I'll just check. Yes, that's fine. Wednesday 11th.

☐ That's fine with me. How do I get to you?

☐ Have you got my email address?

2 Speaking.

☐ I'm looking forward to it. Bye for now.

END-OF-UNIT PUZZLE Find pairs of words to match to the clues below, as in the example. Which word remains alone?

~~maternity~~	short	pension	phone	flexible	human	hours	resources	vitae
job	paid	medical	personnel	course	annual	recruitment	insurance	vacancy
appraisal	agency	curriculum	training	list	plan	holiday	mobile	~~leave~~

1 time off to have a baby ..*maternity leave*.....................................

2 the group of best candidates for a post ....

3 description of a person's career and education ....

4 a plan to cover you in case of sickness ....

5 an organization that finds new people to join companies ....

6 a meeting every year to discuss your work with your manager ....

7 most companies offer four to six weeks of this per year ....

8 a position available in a company ....

9 you can use this to contact people when you are out of the office ....

10 you can choose when you start and finish work each day ....

11 a scheme which pays you money after retirement ....

12 a way of improving your skills ....

13 HR ....

FOCUS ON WORDS: *Customer service*

1   Read this extract from an interview and choose the best word in *italics*.

A   So what do you do to [1] *attract / encourage / make* customer loyalty?

B   We have a [2] *loyalty / fidelity / company* card which we distribute free to all our customers. Every time they buy something, they win points and can get free gifts. It's the best way of getting [3] *again / comeback / repeat* business.

A   And do you have an [4] *online / offline / outline* shopping service?

B   Yes, we do. And we also use our website to [5] *lead / conduct / have* surveys of customer opinion.

A   And how do you [6] *deal / treat / do* with customer complaints?

B   Well, in all our stores we have a special customer service desk. But we also have a call [7] *reception / line / centre* which customers can phone when they have a problem.

A   So customer service is very important to you?

B   Yes, absolutely vital. We want to be sure that we can [8] *meet / respond / accept* the needs of our customers month after month, year after year.

2   Complete the word families in this table, as in the example.

NOUN	VERB	ADJECTIVE
advice	advise	*advisory*
1	✗	loyal
2	invite	3
4	need	5
6	7	satisfied
personalization	8	✗
9	complain	✗
10	refund	✗

3   Now complete these sentences with words from the table, as in the example.

1   There was a sales assistant there to ..*advise*........... me on the best computer to choose.

2   If customers want to .... about our service, thay can call our hotline.

3   Thanks very much for the .... to your product launch.

4   I'm not at all .... with the performance of my new car.

5   If you stay .... to the same supplier, you can often negotiate better conditions.

6   They refused to .... me the money for my watch; they just offered to repair it.

7   The information we get from online surveys allows us to .... our offer of goods and services to our customers.

8   I think we .... a new product to improve our sales.

4 Read this text and decide if the statements below are true (T) or false (F).

TRUSTING THE CUSTOMER

Robert Ritchie's hi-fi business wowed the customer with its trust in the customer and Robert's own enthusiasm.

Robert Ritchie, who sells hi-fi equipment in Angus, Scotland, has been nominated for a 'Wow' award by David Robb. Here's what David had to say:

'I went to the shop on a Saturday looking for some new hi-fi speakers, and hoping to arrange a home demonstration in the next week or two. Not only were they extremely helpful (lots of time taken, coffee provided, etc.), but I went home with two pairs of brand-new speakers, worth over a thousand pounds, to try out, and with no pressure to return them quickly. They did not know me, and refused to accept the deposit I offered.

'This was followed by a visit from Mr Ritchie early on Sunday evening. This was extremely useful in helping me to decide which speaker was best for my room. I still needed time to decide, however, and was allowed to keep them longer with no specific date for their return. I eventually contacted them on Tuesday. They told me to keep the two unwanted speakers until they were next in my area. However, I took them back to the shop on the Wednesday, and paid for the two I had bought. Not only did I get another coffee, but had another hour's relaxed chat with Mr Ritchie, and a demonstration of some equipment which was much too expensive for me but fun to listen to. I left the shop with the feeling that I wasn't a customer, but a friend.

'I told my story on the email forum of a well-known hi-fi manufacturer, and within the hour four or five other messages came in describing similar experiences, over many years, which other people had had with the same Mr Ritchie. The general feeling was that he is the best hi-fi dealer in Scotland.'

www.TheWowAwards.com

1 David Robb took home four speakers. ....
2 He gave the speakers back on the following Monday. ....
3 David visited Mr Ritchie's house. ....
4 Mr Ritchie gave David some more advice on Sunday. ....
5 David bought two pairs of speakers. ....
6 When David returned to the shop, Mr Ritchie gave him another coffee. ....
7 David bought some other more expensive equipment. ....
8 David saw emails from other satisfied customers of Mr Ritchie. ....

(((5.1))) **5** 1 Put the words in this list in the table, as in the example.

| satisfaction | repeat | centre | complain | loyal | encourage | invite |
| professional | guarantee | survey | satisfied | advice | personalized | offer |

2 SYLLABLES

*rep**ea**t*

Clue: four words are stressed on the first syllable, and four on the second.

3 SYLLABLES

Clue: each word is stressed on a different syllable.

4 SYLLABLES

Clue: each word is stressed on a different syllable.

2 Underline the stressed syllable for each word in the table, as in the example. Read the clue at the bottom of each column to help you.
3 Now listen to the words and repeat. Make sure you stress the correct syllable.

FOCUS ON GRAMMAR: *Comparatives and superlatives*

1 Look at this list of adjectives and find twelve pairs of opposites, as in the example.

One word will be left. What is the opposite of this word? ....

better	safer	nearer	the lowest	the easiest
smaller	the oldest	shorter	more	the most expensive
happier	less happy	the youngest	bigger	the most interesting
longer	fewer / less	more dangerous	the highest	further
the most difficult	~~slower~~	the least interesting	~~quicker~~	the cheapest

quicker – slower ....

....

....

....

2 Look at the information in this table and decide if the sentences below are true (T) or false (F). Then correct the false sentences, as in the example.

COUNTRY	TV (PER 100 HOMES)	TELEPHONES (PER 100 PEOPLE)	COST OF LIVING INDEX (USA = 100)	LIFE EXPECTANCY (IN YEARS)	TOBACCO / CIGARETTES PERSON / DAY
Argentina	87.1	20.5	93	72.9	N/A
France	95.7	58.3	117	78.1	N/A
Germany	96.8	56.6	97	77.2	4.6
Italy	94.2	45.6	86	78.2	4.2
Japan	99.3	49.4	138	80.0	7.6
Poland	97.0	22.0	61	72.5	6.4
Spain	87.0	41.7	86	78.0	5.4
UK	98.2	54.9	113	77.2	N/A
USA	98.1	67.7	100	76.7	4.9

N/A = Figures not available

1 Japan has a higher number of TVs than the USA. *T* ....
2 France has fewer telephones than Spain. *F – more telephones* ....
3 Life is cheaper in the UK than in Argentina. ....
4 The French have longer lives than the Spanish. ....
5 The Americans smoke more cigarettes than the Polish. ....
6 TV seems less popular in the north of Europe than in the south. ....
7 Italy has a lower number of telephones than Germany. ....
8 The cost of living is much higher in Argentina than in Japan. ....
9 The Japanese have a better life expectancy than the British. ....
10 The Germans smoke more tobacco than the Spanish. ....

3 Look at the table again. Choose a word from this list to complete the sentences below. Put each word in the appropriate (superlative) form, as in the example.

~~high~~	good	healthy	few	expensive
bad	low	cheap	big	

1 Japan has *the highest* .... number of TVs per 100 homes, and Spain has ....

2 The USA has the most telephones per 100 people, and Argentina has ....

3 Poland is .... country to live in, and Japan is ....

4 Japan has .... life expectancy of the nine countries, and Poland has ....

5 The Japanese are .... smokers of the six countries mentioned.

6 The Italians are perhaps ...., because they don't smoke as much as the other five countries mentioned.

4 Do any of the statistics in **2** surprise you? Write sentences to explain what you find surprising.

e.g. *There are more TVs in the UK than in the USA.*
The USA doesn't have the highest number of TVs in the world.

1 ....
2 ....
3 ....
4 ....

 **5** Listen and answer these questions. You will hear the correct answer after each question.

▶▶▶▶▶ **FOCUS EXTRA:** *Fractions and percentages*

1 Match the words in A to the figures in B.

A		B	
1	just over a fifth	a	49%
2	nearly a third	b	12.5%
3	more than three-quarters	c	22%
4	an eighth	d	70%
5	almost half	e	77%
6	seven-tenths	f	31%

2 Now write these percentages as fractions (½, etc.)

1 66% ....
2 40% ....
3 90% ....
4 52% ....
5 24% ....

FOCUS ON EXPRESSIONS: *Asking for and giving opinions*

1 Choose the correct word in *italics* in sentences 1–6. Then match the sentences to responses a–f.

1 *Are / Do* you agree that we should contact them now?

2 *What /How* do you think about that proposal?

3 *That's / You're* a good point.

4 I *think / don't think* we *should / shouldn't* do anything now.

5 *I'm not / I don't* agree with you.

6 I think *it /so* too.

a So do I. ......
b Yes, it is. ......
c Yes, I do. ......
d I agree with you. It's too early. ......
e Why not? ......
f It seems like a good idea. ......

2 The participants in the meeting below are discussing ideas for improving phone skills. Beate Müller (BM) doesn't agree with the others. Complete the gaps in the dialogue with these expressions.

| I don't think | that's a good point | do you think | I feel |
| do you feel | Don't you think | ~~I think staff should~~ | I agree |

AF If a customer has a complaint, [1] *I think staff should* .... say sorry immediately.

BM I'm sorry, but I don't agree with you at all. If they say sorry, that means it's our fault.

JH Oh, [2] .... so. We're just saying that we are sorry they have a problem. Customers like to hear that.

AF [3] .... with you, John. In a survey we did recently, many of our customers said that the person they spoke to didn't understand the difficulties they were having.

JH What [4] .... about this, Thierry?

TD Well, I take your point about the importance of saying sorry, but [5] .... there's something even more important here. Too many staff are telling customers that there's nothing they can do. They say the problem is the *customer's* fault. That's just not acceptable.

AF Yes, [6] .... I agree entirely. How [7] .... about all this, Beate? Don't you agree?

BM No, I'm afraid I don't. [8] .... that customers sometimes make mistakes too? Some of them try to make *us* pay for *their* mistakes. But I agree that it's important to be polite and listen carefully first.

3 Thierry Dupoué of Socotim has sent the memo below to three of his colleagues. Complete the gaps with these words.

discussion	proposals	Agenda	Minutes
Action points	AOB	Participants	

SOCOTIM

Customer service department

Next meeting on Wednesday 12th April, 10–12 a.m.

1 ....: Thierry Dupoué, Antonio Fernandez, Beate Müller, John Howe

2 ....

1 3 .... of meeting of 8th March

2 Presentation of 4 .... for improving phone skills of call centre staff (JH)

3 General 5 .... on JH's presentation

4 6 .... – who, what and when?

5 7 ....

Please be sure to arrive on time! **TD**

END-OF-UNIT PUZZLE   Read the clues to complete this crossword puzzle. The first letter is given.

1 Where lots of people work using telephones to deal with customers' orders: *c*............ *c*............ .

2 When a customer goes back to a company to buy more, we call this *r*............ business.

3 When I bought my computer, I paid for a service *c* .... in case of problems.

4 If a lot of people use or buy a product or service, we say it is very *p*............ .

5 Women who buy things are *f*............ customers.

6 Big supermarkets give regular customers *l*............ cards.

7 If you make something better, you *i*............ it.

8 When an online company (or a hotel receptionist, a conference organizer, etc.) asks you for your personal details, this procedure is called *r*............ .

9 Older people who use the Internet are called 'silver *s*............'.

10 A service which is always provided on time is a *r*............ service.

FOCUS ON WORDS: *Ordering and delivering*

1 Read this advertisement and choose the correct word in *italics*.

FAST FORWARD

The best in home entertainment ... now at YOUR home in 24 hours

Fast Forward's NEW customer order systems allow us to [1] *process / purchase* your order very quickly. We can now [2] *shipment / ship* your order from our warehouse within the hour and [3] *delivery / deliver* the following day – directly to your door.

- 80,000 CD, DVD and VHS titles in stock, with guaranteed next-day [4] *deliver / delivery* for [5] *orders / quotations* received before 2 p.m.
- Free [6] *ship / shipping* when you [7] *purchase / track* goods more than £30 in value. *
- NEW online [8] *process / tracking* system – follow the progress of your order on our website.

* Valid for UK only. For overseas orders, phone our customer service hotline and ask for an individual [9] *quotation / enquiry*.

2 For each group of verbs in B, underline one verb that *doesn't go* with the noun in A, as in the example.

e.g. 1 we cannot say *to purchase* an order

	A	B
1	an order	to process / to cancel / to place / <u>to purchase</u> / to ship
2	a price	to quote / to track / to check / to pay / to give
3	a product	to send / to deliver / to progress / to enquire about / to order
4	a process	to ship / to speed up / to follow / to explain / to improve
5	a quotation	to ask for / to provide / to send / to prepare / to pay

3 In the sentences below, different customers are phoning suppliers. For each sentence, choose verbs from the corresponding number in **2** to complete the gaps. For example, in 1 choose from *process / cancel / place / ship*.

1 Hello, I'm phoning to .... my order. We've found another supplier who can .... the goods to us tomorrow. Sorry about that, but it is rather urgent.

2 Could I just .... that the unit price is still the same? It is? Good. Can you .... me a price for 150 units, delivery included?

3 I'm calling to .... your FireLine range of products. Is it possible to .... them by phone, or do I need to send a fax?

4 Yes, I know you're waiting for your money, but I'm afraid we can't .... the payment process – there are certain procedures that we always have to ....

5 I forgot to .... a quotation when I spoke to you yesterday. Can you .... one for me and fax it to me here?

Amazon wins new friends

It all started when Amazon promised to deliver the new Harry Potter book on the same day that it first appeared in the shops. All people had to do was to pre-order it by a specified date. It was a huge multiple order – over 250,000 copies – and Amazon and its partner, Federal Express, came very near to fulfilling it.

According to news reports, about 3,800 people did not get their books on time because of a problem with computer software, which misread mailing addresses on some orders. Amazon said that 1.5 per cent of the books did not get to Potter's fans on the big day. In other words, the company scored 98.5 per cent

on keeping its promise. That's not bad, but something even better happened next. Amazon admitted its mistake and apologized – first to its customers and then to reporters who wanted to know how the much-publicized delivery went. Then the company offered to compensate the customers who received late shipment by giving them full refunds of the purchase price – plus shipping and handling – and they could keep their books!

The total cost for Amazon's apology could reach as much as $75,000, but it is a nice gesture, and moreover, it's the key to good customer service. It is about doing the obviously right thing at the right time, without hesitation, and without thinking about short-term costs.

1 Most people received their book — a on the date of publication.
2 There was a computer error, b ordered the book.
3 Amazon declared it was their fault c on the right day.
4 A few thousand people d so some books were sent to the wrong
5 Amazon promised delivery of the book   address.
   book e received their delivery late.
6 Amazon offered 3,800 people f for its customer service.
7 More than 250,000 people g and said sorry for the mistake.
8 Amazon received good publicity h their money back.

5   Look at the complete sentences in 4 again. In what order did the different things happen? For example, The first sentence is *5a* (*Amazon promised delivery of the book on the date of publication*).

5a   ....

FOCUS ON GRAMMAR: *Will and going to*

1 Complete the gaps with these verbs in an appropriate form, as in the example. Use *will* if it's a decision at the moment of speaking, and *going to* if it's an arrangement.

| close   check   try   start   invite   ask   ~~speak~~   launch |

1 A I can't hear you very well.
  B I'm sorry. I ..*'ll speak*.. up a little.
2 Have you heard that they .... another new product in June?
3 A Did you talk to your boss about going part-time?
  B Yes, I did. I .... working three days a week from next month.
4 I'm afraid I can't answer that question. I .... one of my colleagues, then call you back.
5 A Isn't it the fiftieth anniversary of your company this year?
  B Yes, it is. We .... all our customers to a big party in a local hotel.
6 A My order didn't arrive this morning.
  B I do apologize. I .... the details on our order-tracking system.
7 A Would you like to leave a message?
  B No that's OK. I .... again this afternoon.
8 The company .... in June because business has been really bad.

2 Match situations 1–8 with predictions a–h and complete the predictions with the appropriate *going to* form, as in the example.

Situation	Prediction
1 There's not a cloud in the sky.	a I (not get) .... the job.
2 We have to reduce our prices because of our competition.	b It (be) ..*is going to be*.......................... a beautiful day.
3 We've got a few quality problems with our finished products.	c You (not find) .... it easy to work with him.
4 I didn't hear my alarm clock this morning.	d We (get) .... more complaints from customers.
5 The project is running very late.	e I (miss) .... my plane.
6 I didn't do very well at the interview.	f They (not finish) .... on time.
7 We need ten engineers to install the software.	g It (not be) .... cheap to introduce the new technology.
8 Our new boss has a reputation for being strict.	h Our profit margins (fall) ....

(((6.1))) **3** Listen, and answer these questions about your future plans. Use *going to* if you are sure, and *will* if you aren't.

e.g.   **A** *Where are you going tomorrow evening?*
      B *I'm going to meet a friend for a drink.*
      C *I'll probably eat out in a restaurant.*
      D *Perhaps I'll stay at home and watch TV.*

4 Here are some famous predictions. The sentences below them explain what they mean. Complete each sentence with *will* or *won't*, as in the example.

1 'There will never be a bigger plane built.'
It ..*will*.............................. be impossible to design a larger one.

2 'It will be years – not in my time – before a woman will become Prime Minister.'
There .... be a woman Prime Minister in my lifetime.

3 'There is no reason anyone would want a computer in their home.'
There .... be a domestic market for computers.

4 'There is not the slightest indication that nuclear energy will ever be obtainable.'
There is no proof that it .... be possible to produce nuclear power.

5 'No one will pay good money to get from Berlin to Potsdam in one hour when he can ride his horse there in one day for free.'
People .... want to pay to travel because horses are free.

6 'The Americans have need of the telephone, but we do not. We have plenty of messenger boys.'
We .... continue to communicate by messenger boy.

5 Now match the predictions 1–6 in **4** to the people a–f who said them.

a   Ken Olson, President of Digital Equipment Corp, 1977 ....
b   King William I of Prussia on hearing of the invention of trains ....
c   A Boeing engineer, after the first flight of the 247, a twin-engine plane that carried ten people ....
d   Sir William Preece, Chief Engineer, British Post Office, 1876 ....
e   Margaret Thatcher, 1974 ....
f   Albert Einstein, 1932 ....

FOCUS ON EXPRESSIONS: *Giving bad news and saying sorry*

1   Complete the gaps in the dialogues below with these expressions.

Shall I call the transporter	I'll do what I can	I'm sorry
I'm very sorry to hear that	I'm afraid	Shall I send you
We'll deal with it	that's OK	if you could
that's a bit annoying		

A   Can you ship the products to us in the next couple of days?

B   Well, they're still in production, so [1]... it won't be before the end of the week.

A   Well, [2].. .

B   Yes, I do apologize for the delay. We received a lot of big orders at the same time.

A   So, do you think we can have them for Friday?

B   [3].. , but I can't promise anything.

C   I'm trying to track a shipment on your website, but I always get an error message.

D   Yes. [4].. , but we're having a few problems with it today.

C   Could you check if my order left the factory yesterday? The order reference is BS857.

D   One moment ...Yes, it did. [5].. and find out where it is now?

C   No, [6].. . If it's on its way, that's fine.

D   OK, and I'm sorry again about the website problem. [7].. as soon as we can.

E   Did you receive the shipment this morning?

F   Yes, we did, but two of the boxes were already open.

E   Oh, [8].. . Did you check the contents?

F   Yes, they're all there, but some of them are broken.

E   I do apologize for that. I'll have a word with our delivery driver. [9].. two replacement boxes today?

F   Yes, please, [10].. .

(((6.2))) **2**   Listen to three people describing their problems. For each dialogue, answer these questions.

   a   What's the problem?

   b   What's the cause of the problem?

   c   How do they solve the problem?

3 This is an email to accompany a late quotation. Put the parts of the email in the correct order 1–12. The first and last are done for you.

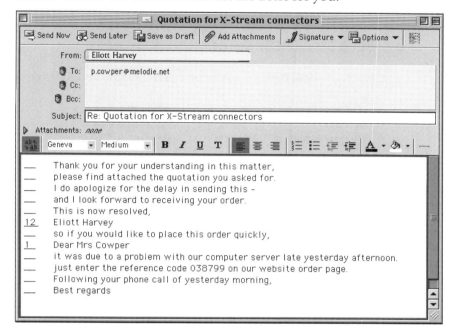

Quotation for X-Stream connectors

Send Now Send Later Save as Draft Add Attachments Signature ▼ Options ▼

From: Eliott Harvey
To: p.cowper@melodie.net
Cc:
Bcc:
Subject: Re: Quotation for X-Stream connectors
Attachments: none

Geneva ▼ Medium ▼ **B** *I* <u>U</u> T

___ Thank you for your understanding in this matter,
___ please find attached the quotation you asked for.
___ I do apologize for the delay in sending this –
___ and I look forward to receiving your order.
___ This is now resolved,
_12_ Eliott Harvey
___ so if you would like to place this order quickly,
_1_ Dear Mrs Cowper
___ it was due to a problem with our computer server late yesterday afternoon.
___ just enter the reference code 038799 on our website order page.
___ Following your phone call of yesterday morning,
___ Best regards

END-OF-UNIT PUZZLE

1 Find twelve words in the snake. The last letter of each word is the first letter of the next word, e.g. stockeep → stock keep.

2 Now complete sentences 1-11 with words from the snake.

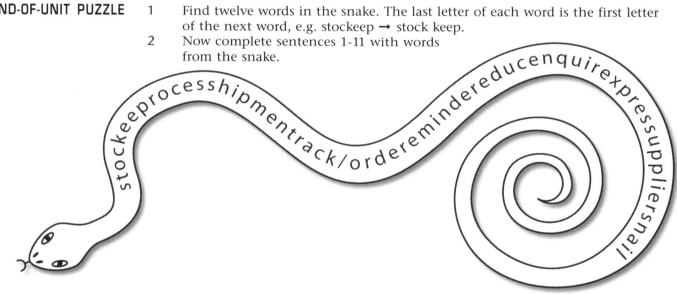

1 We always negotiate the best possible prices from our ....
2 Finished goods that you store in your company are called ....
3 Letters sent by post are now often called ...... mail.
4 We ...... a very high level of stock because our customers want immediate delivery.
5 If you want to send goods quickly, you use an ...... delivery service like UPS.
6 I'm phoning to ...... about your products.
7 Goods which are being transported: ....
8 If you follow the progress of a shipment online, you ...... your ....
9 If a customer hasn't paid, you send them a ....
10 We should try to ...... the amount of paper we use in our offices.
11 It takes us about four hours to ...... an order from a customer.

FOCUS ON WORDS: *Company structure*

1 Match the departments in the box to the definitions 1–9 below.

Quality control	Legal	Accounts
Marketing	Production	Public Relations
Human Resources	Sales	Research & Development

1 They give information to the press. ....
2 The people who pay the bills and receive money. ....
3 The division which makes the goods in the factory. ....
4 The department which checks the finished goods. ....
5 They run tests and make prototypes. ....
6 These people are responsible for promotion and advertising. ....
7 This department sells the products to the customers. ....
8 They recruit staff and organize training. ....
9 This department organizes contracts. ....

2 Read this letter confirming a job appointment and choose the correct word in *italics*.

Dear Ms Tan,

I am pleased to confirm your appointment as a laboratory technician in our Research Department. As you know, the department is [1]*division / divided / part* into three business units. You will work [2]*in / to / on* the detergents unit, where you will be [3]*responsible / charge / work* for laboratory trials. You will [4]*relate / respond / report* directly to Dr Martins, who is in [5]*responsible to / charge of / head of* the development of our next generation of detergents. There are thirty-five [6]*staff / personnel / persons* working in your unit.

We wish you a long and successful career working [7]*by / on / for* our company.

Yours sincerely,

Erica D'Arcy

[8]*Head / Responsible / Manager* of Personnel

3 Put these letters in the correct order to make the names of eight jobs.

1	rotcdo	*...doctor...*	5	yewral	....
2	aatncuoctn	....	6	reivrd	....
3	niptrctsioee	....	7	niarter	....
4	yrscetare	....	8	regnmaa	....

4 Read this text about Dassault Aviation and decide if the sentences 1–8 below are true (T) or false (F).

Dassault Aviation is famous all over the world for designing and building high-performance aircraft for military and business use. With sales of over 3,000,000,000 euros, Dassault is one of France's most successful companies. Its main product is the Falcon business jet. In 2000 it had a 45% share of this market, with 66% of its civil sales in the United States. It has nine sites in France, its headquarters in Paris, and offices in four other continents. In France the main site is in St Cloud near Paris. Over 2,800 employees work there in the Research Centre and also in the other departments such as Sales, Logistics, IT, Marketing, Finance and HR.

The company has two main divisions which correspond to its two main markets: Defence Division (combat aircraft) and Falcon Division for business jets. About 70% of the sales are in the business jet division. All assembly for both divisions takes place at Merignac in South West France. The other seven plants are responsible for a particular activity such as wing or tail construction or machining parts.

Four of the sites are in the Defence Division and three in the Falcon Division. Each plane flies for the first time at Merignac.

The group has two major stockholders, Groupe Industriel Marcel Dassault and EADS. Dassault has just over 50% of the shares, EADS owns just under 46% and minority shareholders own the other 4%. The Executive Committee has eleven members including the Chairman and CEO, Mr Charles Edelstenne.

Dassault has military customers in over twenty countries and business customers in nearly forty. Over the next few years they will continue to invest in research particularly for the new generation of Rafale combat aircraft, the future executive jet Falcon 7X and pilotless combat aircraft.

1 Dassault constructs and sells aircraft. ....
2 The group is based in Paris. ....
3 The main site is in Germany. ....
4 The company has three main divisions. ....
5 Sales are higher in the military division. ....
6 All planes make their first flight at St Cloud. ....
7 Charles Edelstenne is the major shareholder. ....
8 The company plans to stop investment. ....

5 How do you say these numbers from the text?

1 46%
2 3,000,000,000
3 2000
4 2,800

(((7.1))) **6** Listen to this description of the Dutch firm ING. Are these statements true (T) or false (F)?

1 ING is a computer services firm. ....
2 About 7,500 people visit the head office every year. ....
3 The head office consists of ten towers. ....
4 The buildings don't have any rectangular rooms. ....
5 The company is constructing new office buildings. ....
6 The Chairman doesn't think that office buildings are important for a company's image. ....
7 The Chairman gives a present to all his employees at Christmas. ....
8 ING wants to keep the culture of a small company. ....

FOCUS ON GRAMMAR: *Question types*

1 Read this factfile about Grohe and make questions for the answers below, as in the example.

GROHE

Headquarters: Hemer, Germany

Products: taps for bathrooms, kitchens, etc.

Well-known brand: Grohe Water Technology (launched in mid-1990s)

Production facilities: 8 in Germany, 1 each in Portugal, Thailand, Canada

Employees: 5,900

Present strategy:

– to become more efficient and autonomous: the company went private in 2000

– to develop international markets (the German market is 5% down)

---

1 What *does Grohe produce* .... ?
   Taps.
2 *Where* .... ?
   Hemer.
3 *When* .... ?
   In the mid-90s.
4 *How many* .... ?
   Eight.
5 *Where* .... ?
   In Germany, Portugal, Thailand and Canada.
6 *Why* .... ?
   Because the German construction market is 5% down.
7 *When* .... ?
   In 2000.
8 *How many* .... ?
   About 5,900.

2 Read this interview with an employee of Boeing and complete the gaps with the questions in the box, as in the example.

> Which department are you working in?
> Why did you choose Boeing?
> You graduated in Communications, didn't you?
> How does that work?
> Does it have a good reputation, then?
> ~~When did you join the company?~~
> You work in the Commercial Airplanes Division, don't you?
> You are in the Business Career Foundation Program, aren't you?
> Do you have any contacts with the leadership of Boeing?
> Is that interesting?

I ¹ *When did you join the company?* ....

M I joined last year.

I ² ....

M Yes, I did. From Seattle Pacific University.

I ³ ....

M Because it's the best constructor in the industry.

I ⁴ ....

M Yes, it does. Excellent in fact.

I ⁵ ....

M Yes, I do. At least for the moment.

I ⁶ ....

M At the moment I'm in Cost Accounting.

I ⁷ ....

M Yes it is. It's interesting to see how different departments at Boeing work.

I ⁸ ....

M Yes, I am.

I ⁹ ....

M I work in six different departments over a two-year period: four months in Cost Accounting, four months in Design, and so on.

I Sounds great. ¹⁰ ....

M Yes, we do. We have mentors who are executives in the company. Mine, for example, is the Director of Human Resources.

I Well, good luck with the rest of the program.

3 Complete these sentences with an appropriate question tag.

1 You're Swiss, *aren't you* ....?

2 You live in Lugano, ... ?

3 It's in the Italian part of Switzerland, ... ?

4 You're a lawyer, ... ?

5 You speak English, ... ?

6 You can sign these documents, ... ?

7 Your wife's Spanish, ... ?

8 She paints, ... ?

FOCUS ON EXPRESSIONS: *Presenting information*

1 Look at this introduction to a presentation and put the sentences in a logical order 1–10, as in the examples.

☐ I will be happy to take questions at the end.

1 Good afternoon everybody.

☐ I work for GSK in Milan where I am in charge of marketing.

☐ Then we will look at the chewing gum market in general.

☐ My talk will last about 20 minutes and is in two parts.

☐ Is that all clear? OK, let's start.

☐ Firstly, I'm going to talk about the history of the company.

☐ Right. Let's have a look at the first slide.

2 My name is Lorenza Colombo.

☐ Your manager invited me here today to tell you about Wrigley and the chewing-gum market.

《 7.2 》 2 Listen to this presentation about Wrigley and complete the missing information.

1891 William Wrigley Jr arrives in Chicago and sells 1............................ and baking powder, and offers chewing gum free as an incentive.

1892 Sees that chewing gum is a better product and starts selling it under his own name.

1893 Launches 2............................ .

1910 Opens production facilities in 3............................ followed by Australia in 1915.

4............. Company begins construction of Wrigley Building.

1939 First appearance of 5............................ as an advertising idea.

1944 All Wrigley chewing gum stocks sold to the 6............................ .

1991 Start of factory in Guangzhou, 7............................ .

1999 New factory in St Petersburg.

2002 US total sales of chewing gum reach 8............................ – 9............................ sticks per person / year. Wrigley has about 10............................ % of this market.

3 Replace the underlined expressions in these sentences with an expression from the box which has the same meaning.

reached a high	rose	stabilized
increased dramatically	decreased rapidly	increased by 100%

1 Share prices <u>fell sharply</u> this morning. ....

2 Inflation <u>levelled off</u> at 3% in October. ....

3 Cost of sales <u>grew</u> by 2% last year. ....

4 The exchange rate <u>shot up</u> last month. ....

5 Our exports <u>peaked</u> at 20 million in 2001. ....

6 We <u>doubled</u> our domestic sales last year. ....

4 Complete the extracts below from a presentation on Wrigley with these words.

| see | here | begin | look | shows | slide |

I'd like to ¹ .... by telling you a little about the company.
This slide ² .... shows the key years in the history of Wrigley starting with its foundation in 1892 and ending here in 2002 with US sales at 2 billion dollars.

If we look a little more closely, we can see some key strategic decisions.
In 1910 we started building our first factory outside the US and this was followed over the next eighty years by plants in many different countries. As you can ³ .... we now have fourteen factories worldwide from here in China over to Russia and down here in Australasia.

Now, have a ⁴ .... at this. Here we can see the main brands of the Wrigley company from Juicy Fruit introduced in 1893, to Orbit which was launched in 2001.
This pie chart ⁵ .... that Wrigley has about half of all sales in the world despite competition from at least twenty other manufacturers in the US alone.

My next ⁶ .... gives you some information about our flagship building which was started in 1920. It shows the white building lit up at night. This building is a symbol to many Americans of Chicago and the Wrigley company and, as such, is one of the best marketing ventures ever.

END-OF-UNIT PUZZLE Look at this layout of a meeting. Use the clues below to decide where the people on the left sat, as in the example.

CEO – Priscilla Jarman
Sales Director – Hilary Maine
CFO – Malcolm Dillon
Chairman's PA – Tony Evans
Chairman – Peter Sing
Head of IT – Nick Silins
HR Director – Joe Grand
Company lawyer – Dick Clarke
Production Director – Becky Piper
R & D Director – Cameron Kirkby

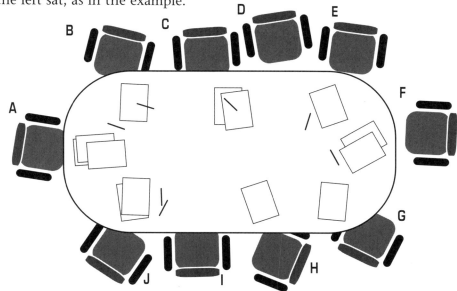

1 The Chairman sat at the head of the table (A) with his PA on his left (B).
2 The CFO sat at the other end of the table with the Sales Director on his left and the company lawyer on the other side.
3 Joe was between Dick and Cameron.
4 Nick sat next to Priscilla and opposite Cameron.
5 Becky and Hilary were next to each other on the same side of the table as Priscilla, with Hilary on Becky's right.

Entertaining
Food and drink

FOCUS ON WORDS: *Eating out*

1   Look at these groups of words and circle the odd one out, as in the example.

1 knife	fork	(napkin)	spoon
2 banana	bean	pear	grape
3 cut	fry	roast	grill
4 chicken	pork	rabbit	salmon
5 soup	apple pie	ice cream	fruit salad
6 glass	plate	cup	mug
7 milk	butter	asparagus	cheese
8 tea	champagne	wine	beer
9 lettuce	tomato	cucumber	pineapple

2   Complete the dialogues below with these adjectives.

crunchy	spicy	sweet	greasy
healthy	simple	filling	tasty

A   Are you having the chocolate cake with ice cream?

B   No, it's too ¹ .... for my taste.

C   What sort of food do you like?

D   I like Italian food. It's very ² .... Just pasta and a sauce.

C   What about Indian?

D   Oh no! It's much too ³ .... for me.

E   Do you like salads?

F   Not really. I know they are very ⁴ .... but I don't think they are very
⁵ .... I prefer stronger flavours, like a good fry-up.

E   What do you mean, exactly?

F   Eggs, bacon, sausages – all fried together. Excellent.

E   Sounds a bit ⁶ .... to me! All that oil. I prefer some nice ⁷ .... carrots –
raw, with beetroot and tomatoes and a good dressing.

F   Not very ⁸ .... though. I'd be hungry again ten minutes later!

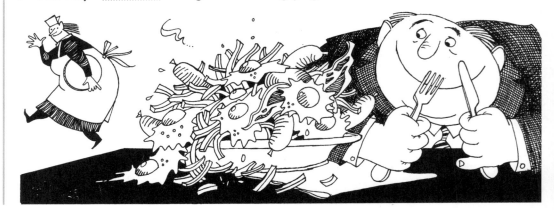

Listen to this story about a very generous host. Are these statements true (T) or false (F)?

1 The businessman works in Germany. ....

2 He was in a London nightclub. ....

3 He wanted to buy the DJ a drink for his birthday. ....

4 He wanted to buy everybody a drink. ....

5 He ordered a glass of champagne for himself. ....

Listen again and match 1–10 to a–j.

1 £4,734.35   a cost of a round of drinks

2 9   b number of hours to complete the order

3 £250   c total cost of the bill for the evening

4 200   d total number of bottles bought

5 £86.50   e cost of a bottle of Jack Daniel's

6 168   f numbers of bottles of champagne ordered

7 £42,000   g cost of the tip

8 3   h number of credit card slips signed

9 11   i number of people present

10 £42,608.25   j cost of a bottle of champagne

5 Find two words that correspond to each of the definitions 1–12 below. Use each word once only.

glass	grape	dinner	grill
		cheese	
white	duck		butter
service	waitress	fry	
red	cucumber		strawberry
	cloth	chef	lunch
chicken		yogurt	
cup			
leg	lettuce	ham	charge

1 two people who work in a restaurant ....

2 two types of fruit ....

3 two types of poultry ....

4 two colours of wine ....

5 two words that go with 'table' ....

6 two types of burger ....

7 two meal times ....

8 two things to drink from ....

9 two salad items ....

10 two ways of cooking ....

11 two dairy products ....

12 extra money you pay on your bill in a restaurant ....

FOCUS ON GRAMMAR: *1st and 2nd conditionals*

1 It is late March. Two people are planning a fund-raising event. Look at these notes and answer the questions below.

Objective
Invite best customers to a day of activities to raise money for charity

Dates

April 7th	April is usually wet
May 15th	same day as national football Cup Final day
July 18th	some customers already on holiday

Costs

Paintball	€10 per person (one hour)
Sailing	€25 per person (one hour)
Treasure hunt	€15 per person (three hours)
Crossbow shooting	€8 per person (one hour)
Laser fight	€10 per person (one hour)
Lunch	€10 per head (buffet); €20 per head (hot meal)

Numbers

Certain	30
Probable	40
Possible	30
Entry fee per person	€100

1 Which is the worst date to do outdoor activities? ....
2 What are the cheapest and most expensive events? ....
3 How many possible activities are there? ....
4 How many customers are definitely coming? ....
5 How much does it cost to attend the event? ....
6 How much is lunch per person? ....

2

1 Match 1–4 to a–d to form some sentences about the event in **1**.

1 We will have an income of €3,000,   a some people will be on holiday.
2 If we don't send the invitations soon,   b if the 'certainties' come.
3 If we organize it in April,   c it will probably rain.
4 If we wait until July,   d nobody will come.

2 Match 5–8 to e–h to form some more sentences about the event in **1**.

5 If we chose the buffet lunch,   e if we organized it in Florida.
6 We would have much better weather   f very few people would come.
7 We would have an income of €10,000   g if everybody came.
8 If we held it on the football   h it would be cheaper for us and
  Cup Final day,   we'd raise more money.

3 Listen to two colleagues discussing the event and complete these sentences.

1 If I .... you, ... a maximum of three.

2 If thirty people ...., how much .... ?

3 €100 each, so if ...., we'll ....

4 If we ...., a lot of people ....

5 Yes, but .... the Cup Final if we ....

6 If .... the three cheapest events, ... €28 per person.

7 If everybody .... , we .... €10,000.

4 Decide if these conditional sentences are likely or unlikely, and complete them with an appropriate form of the verb in brackets, as in the examples.

1 Sandra and I usually travel on the same bus, so if I (get) _get_................ my normal bus today, I _'ll probably_................ (probably see) her.

2 At the annual marketing conference, Pablo and I always find time to play golf. If he (go) .... to the marketing conference again this year, I .... (play) golf with him again.

3 We have house guests this weekend, so I won't have time to finish the report, but if I (not have) .... visitors, I .... (finish) it in time for Monday.

4 A Russian visitor is coming to the company, and I speak Russian, so if he (not speak English) .... , I (translate) .... for you.

5 I work for a large company, and it's not easy to communicate with the managers. If I (work) .... for a small firm, I .... (speak) regularly to my boss.

6 I earn £40,000 a year and live in a £180,000 flat. If I only (earn) .... £20,000 a year, I (not have) .... enough money to pay for it.

5 Complete these sentences about yourself.

1 If I go on holiday this year, ...
2 If I get a salary increase, ...
3 If I met a famous film star, ...
4 If I had more free time, ...

FOCUS ON EXPRESSIONS: *Likes and dislikes*

1 Complete the missing words in these dialogues, as in the example.

A Could I have a [1] *table* _____ for five, please?

B I'm sorry but the restaurant is [2] f _____ at the moment.

A Could we come back later?

B Certainly, sir. What time shall I make the [3] r _____ for?

C Are you ready to [4] o _____ ?

D Yes, please.

C What would you like as a [5] s _____ ?

D We'll both have the soup.

C And for your [6] m _____ c _____ ?

D I'd like the stroganoff.

E And I'll have the vegetarian lasagne.

F Could I have the [7] b _____ , please?

G Certainly. Was everything satisfactory?

F Fine, thank you. Can I pay by [8] c _____ c _____ ?

G Of course.

F And could you call us a [9] t _____ ?

G Of course. Where to?

F The Bath Hotel. Is [10] s _____ included in this bill?

G Yes, it is.

F There you are.

G Thank you very much.

2 What would you say in these situations?

1 You arrive at the restaurant. You have a reservation in your name.

_____

2 There's no menu on your table.

_____

3 You do not know what the 'dish of the day' is. Ask the waiter.

_____

4 You want to know what your friend is going to have.

_____

5 You are now ready to order. Tell the waiter.

_____

6 Your fish is a little undercooked. Tell the waiter.

_____

7 You want some salt.

_____

8 You want to pay.

_____

3 Complete these sentences using the words in brackets, as in the example.

1 A gourmet (love) *loves eating good food* .
2 A bookworm (keen) ....
3 A football fan (love) ....
4 My boss (can't stand) ....
5 One of my friends (fond) ....

4 Make sentences about your tastes and preferences in these different areas of interest, as in the example.

1 (holidays) I love *lying on the beach all afternoon* .
2 (food) I like ....
3 (after work) I prefer .... to ....
4 (jobs around the house) I don't mind ....
5 (films or music) I'm not keen on ....
6 (activities at work) I hate ....

END-OF-UNIT PUZZLE How many questions can you answer in this quiz? The answers are upside down at the bottom of the quiz.

Tick (✔) the best answer.

1 What word is from Gaelic and means 'water of life'?
  a rum   **b** wine   **c** whisky

2 What vegetable is used to make French fries?
  a onion   **b** potato   **c** parsnip

3 What is the missing word in this Beatles' song: '........ fields forever'?
  a Gooseberry   **b** Blackcurrant   **c** Strawberry

4 What large bird has the same name as a country in English?
  a eagle   **b** turkey   **c** pheasant

5 What fruit is also the name of a colour?
  a pineapple   **b** orange   **c** lemon

6 What are Bordeaux and Chianti famous for?
  a wine   **b** coffee   **c** mineral water

7 What did Dom Perignon invent?
  a cider   **b** champagne   **c** brandy

8 What connects Parma and Bayonne?
  a ham   **b** cheese   **c** butter

9 What pie is America famous for?
  a cherry   **b** pumpkin   **c** peach

10 What meat is New Zealand famous for?
  a pork   **b** beef   **c** lamb

11 What alcoholic drink is associated with Japan?
  a tequila   **b** sake   **c** ouzo

12 What are San Pellegrino and Perrier famous for?
  a orange juice   **b** iced tea   **c** mineral water

13 What vegetable makes you cry?
  a green pepper   **b** onion   **c** leek

1c 2b 3c 4b 5b 6a 7b 8a 9b 10c 11b 12c 13b

51

Taking part in meetings
Advertising and selling

FOCUS ON WORDS: *Advertising and promotions*

1   A reporter is interviewing a Marketing Manager about her company's new product. Complete the dialogue with these words and then decide what the product is.

slogan	benefit	single	feature	commercials
billboards	campaign	advertise	target	advertising

A   So the new product is called 'Complicity'?

B   Yes, that's right.

A   Can you tell us about the advertising [1]... ?

B   Yes, of course. We're going to [2].. on TV. We're also doing a lot of outdoor [3].. , especially on [4].. and in bus shelters.

A   So who are the main [5].. groups?

B   We're particularly interested in the 18–30 age range.

A   [6].. people, you mean?

B   No, not only. Married couples, too. People who'll love eating out of the same pot!

A   Oh, so it's a product you share with someone?

B   Yes, that's right. Our campaign [7].. is 'Share the secret, share the pleasure'. One special [8].. of the product is that it comes with two plastic spoons. So it is clearly designed as a product for two people to share.

A   That's very original. How many flavours does it come in?

B   Well, each pot contains six different flavours: Cool Vanilla, Big Banana, Calypso Chocolate, and so on, and you can choose between three different flavour combinations. The real [9].. of this to the customer is that they are sure to find at least one flavour they really like. We've researched this very carefully.

A   I'm sure you have. So when are we going to see the first [10].. on TV?

B   The week after next.

2 Find words in this grid that correspond to the definitions below, as in the example. You can read the words horizontally (left to right) or vertically (top to bottom).

P	O	S	A	M	P	L	E	R	F
R	Y	T	K	M	U	E	T	G	E
I	G	F	I	C	S	A	L	E	S
N	B	W	O	R	D	F	N	N	S
T	A	N	S	X	A	L	L	E	P
E	N	P	K	T	S	E	S	R	O
D	N	H	O	W	B	T	M	A	N
L	E	V	I	D	E	O	Z	L	S
B	R	O	C	H	U	R	E	K	O
V	J	R	O	U	T	D	O	O	R

1 This little book gives detailed information about your products and services. _brochure_

2 Manufacturers sometimes give you a free .... in the supermarket to try at home.

3 This small publicity document is designed to go easily in an envelope or through a letterbox. ....

4 This is a small shop open at the front, where you can buy newspapers, drinks, etc. ....

5 When a customer says good things about your company to another person, we call this ....-of-mouth publicity.

6 When an advert appears in the shop where you buy a product, we call this point-of-.. advertising.

7 Companies often make a promotional .... to show in shops or at trade fairs.

8 When a company pays the costs of a sporting event, we say it is a .... of the event.

9 A product can be sold in the professional or industrial market, or to the .... public.

10 Posters on bus shelters, kiosks or billboards are examples of .... advertising.

11 An advertisement on the Internet is called a .... advert.

(((9.1))) **3** Where is the main stress on these words? Listen and put them in the correct column, as in the examples. Then listen and repeat the words.

billboard	benefits	advertisement	brochures	campaign
features	advertise	samples	consumer	promotional
commercial	sponsorship		target	advertising

Oo	oO	Ooo	oOo	Oooo	oOoo
billboard		_benefits_			

FOCUS ON GRAMMAR: *Modals of obligation and permission*

1 Read this information on 'Telemarketing and you'. Then choose the correct word in *italics* to complete the text below.

Telemarketing and you

How are you protected?

MR BURNS, WOULD YOU LIKE THE CHANCE TO WIN DINNER FOR TWO AT MAXIM'S RESTAURANT?

1 You have the right to ask a company to stop making phone calls to your home.

2 Companies are required to keep 'do-not-call' lists for 10 years (but this is not necessary for non-profit organizations such as charities). It is illegal for a telemarketer to call you if you have asked not to be called.

3 Telemarketing calls are only possible between 8 a.m. and 9 p.m.

4 Telemarketers must give you the name of the seller, and what they are selling. If they are offering you the chance to win a prize in a competition, they are required to tell you that the competition is free to everybody and that there is no obligation to buy something.

You ¹ *can / can't* ask a company not to phone your home.

The company ² *can / must* keep a 'do-not-call' list for 10 years, and ³ *is allowed to / mustn't* make any more sales calls to you during this time.

Non-profit organizations ⁴ *mustn't / don't have to* keep these lists.

Telemarketers ⁵ *are allowed to / mustn't* call you between 8 a.m. and 9 p.m., but they ⁶ *can't / have to* ring outside these hours.

Telemarketers ⁷ *aren't allowed to / have to* tell you which company they represent and what they are selling. If there is a prize on offer, they ⁸ *must / can't* inform you that everybody ⁹ *has to / is allowed to* enter the competition and you ¹⁰ *mustn't / don't have to* buy something first.

2 Complete the dialogue with these expressions.

do you have to	have to	are you allowed	can't
are allowed	can	don't have to	doesn't have to
isn't allowed	does he have to	has to	can he

A How many hours a week are you doing in this new job?

B Oh, probably about fifty-five or sixty.

A That's a lot. So ¹........................... work at weekends sometimes?

B No, I don't. But I often ²........................... work late in the evenings, because that's the only time I get to answer my emails.

A What about holidays? ³........................... to take them when you want?

B No, I'm not. I ⁴........................... take any holiday from mid-July to mid-August, because I'm single. Only employees with children ⁵........................... to take time off in that period.

A Is that a problem, then?

B No, not at all. I like it. It means that I 6.. go on holiday in June
or September when flights and hotels are cheaper.

A And you 7.. share the beach or swimming pool with hundreds
of schoolchildren!

B Yes, that's right. What about Ken? How's he doing in his new advertising job?

A He's really enjoying it. He 8.. do the same hours as you because
he's only working part-time. But he 9.. to take any holiday this
summer, because he's just started. He'll have to wait until Christmas, now.

B And 10.. travel a lot?

A No, not much. He's more in the design field, so he 11.. spend
most of his time in front of a computer. But that's OK, because it's only three days
a week.

B So 12.. choose the days he doesn't work?

A No, that's not possible. The company always want him on Monday, Tuesday and
Wednesday.

3 Make true sentences about your job, using the verbs from 2.

e.g. *I'm not allowed to take my holidays when I want.*
   I sometimes have to work at weekends.

1 I .... take my holidays when I want.

2 I .... work at weekends.

3 I .... work late in the evening.

4 I .... travel a lot for my work.

5 I .... spend a lot of time in front of the computer.

6 I .... go for lunch when I want.

7 I .... use English at work.

▶ ▶ ▶ ▶ **FOCUS EXTRA**   *I really must ...*

We use *I really must ...* when we need to take action quickly. Complete these sentences
in an appropriate way, as in the example.

1 My appointment's in half an hour. It's twenty minutes away in the car.
   I really must leave now.. .

2 My spoken English isn't very good.
   I really must ....

3 One of my suppliers always delivers late. I've complained to them several times.
   I really must ....

4 It's my wife's / husband's / friend's birthday tomorrow.
   I really must ....

5 My computer crashes two or three times every day.
   I really must ....

6 I have a lot of work, and I'm feeling really tired these days.
   I really must ....

FOCUS ON EXPRESSIONS: *Managing discussions and describing trends*

1 Read this dialogue from a meeting and choose the correct word or expression in *italics*.

A OK, everybody. Thank you ¹ *to come / for come / for coming*. I hope you had a good lunch. We'll just wait a few minutes for Danni. He's finishing his coffee.

B So what's on the agenda for today?

A Well, I thought we could maybe discuss our advertising.

C Sorry, I'm not ² *agree / with you / follow*. What aspect of our advertising?

B Yes, could you be more ³ *detailed / specific / apparent*?

A Well, you received the six-monthly report I sent you?

B/C No, we didn't.

A Well, I did send it to you! Perhaps you can read it this evening, then we can ⁴ *return / call / come back* to this point in tomorrow's meeting.

B Sorry, I ⁵ *didn't / 'm not / don't* catch that. Did you say there's a meeting tomorrow?

A Yes, that's right, Bridget. But we're wasting time here. Can we ⁶ *pass / move on / target* to the next point on the agenda?

B And what is the next point?

A It's about the new sales position ... Ah, Hello, Danni. Take a seat.

D Thanks. Sorry to be late. Can you just quickly ⁷ *go / return / speak* over what you've been discussing?

C Well, we haven't really started yet!

2 You are chairing a meeting. Decide what you would say in these situations. Complete the gaps, then check your answers in the Answer Key on page 78.

1 You want to begin the meeting.
OK, ...*everybody's*.. here. Can we ...*start*..?

2 You didn't hear what someone said.
Sorry, I didn't .... Could you say it again?

3 You don't understand what someone is trying to say.
Sorry, I'm .... you. .... more specific?

4 You think someone is changing the subject.
That's not really on .... for today. Can we
.... to that another time?

5 You want to change to a new subject.
I think we've .... that point. Can we
.... to the next item on the agenda?

6 You want to close the meeting.
OK. That's .... for today. Can we .... what we've agreed?

1 Listen to some people at a meeting responding to the sentences in **2**. Match the responses to the original sentences, as in the example.

1 ..*a*...... 2 .... 3 .... 4 .... 5 ..*b*...... 6 ....

2 Now listen to the complete dialogues and check your answers.

4 Look at this graph and choose the correct word in *italics* to complete the description.

Source: http://www.adassoc.org.uk/press/press70_stats.html

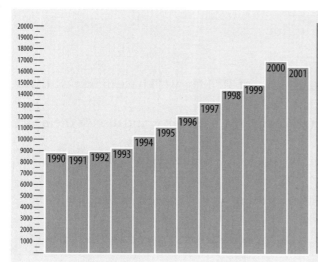

Total adspend in 1990 was just under £9,000m. It ¹ *fell / rose* in 1991 ² *to / by* about £8,500m, then it went up again ³ *by / to* about £400m in the following year. In 1993 spending ⁴ *increased / decreased* again ⁵ *slightly / dramatically*, but in the next year it ⁶ *rose / dropped* more ⁷ *sharply / slightly*, reaching over £10,000m in 1994. In the next two years to 1996, expenditure continued to go up ⁸ *steadily / slightly*, increasing ⁹ *by / from* about £1,000m each year. In 1997 it rose ¹⁰ *steadily / sharply* by £1,300m, but the rate of increase ¹¹ *went up / dropped* again in 1998, with a rise of only £1,000m. There was a similar ¹² *rise / fall* in 1999 and 2000, with adspend increasing to ¹³ *stand at / drop* at about £17,000m, before falling slightly in 2001.

END-OF-UNIT PUZZLE

Put the letters in the words in brackets in the right order to complete the funny stories about advertising.

aphrodisiac: a substance that increases sexual desire

ancestors: family members who lived before your grandparents

grave: a hole in the ground where you put people's bodies when they die

1 Colgate had big problems when it tried to (*rotpeom*) .... its toothpaste in certain countries. In Spanish, the verb 'colgar' means to hang (in the sense of execution by a rope round the neck). So 'Colgate' translates into the command 'go and hang yourself'.

2 When Kentucky Fried Chicken (*auclhnde*) .... its first promotional campaign in China, it used its famous (*lgsnoa*) .... 'finger-lickin' good'. In the local language, this translated as 'eat your fingers off'.

3 Guinness is considered an aphrodisiac in some African countries. For this reason, it is (*mrkeated*) .... under the slogan 'a baby in every bottle'.

4 Pepsi launched an advertising (*amacipgn*) .... in China with its slogan 'Come alive with the Pepsi generation'. In Chinese, this meant 'Pepsi brings your ancestors back from the grave'.

10 Managing your time
Projects and processes

FOCUS ON WORDS: *Project and time management*

1 Choose a word from the box to complete the gaps in the sentences below, as in the example.

> task   results   time   ~~deadline~~
> record   progress   meeting

1 If we want to meet the ...*deadline*............ of 31st May, we'll have to take on more people to help us finish the job.
2 We keep a .... of all complaints we receive, and discuss them at the end of each month.
3 Now that we're halfway through the project, we should meet to review ....
4 We didn't have time to talk about everything, so we'll have to schedule another .... for next week.
5 We'll evaluate the .... of the tests when they come back from the research laboratory.
6 We'll need someone to monitor the .... spent on every step in the production process.
7 Can you complete that .... before you start another one!

2 Complete this table, as in the example.

| VERB | [1]to analyse | to deliver | [3] | to decide on | [5] | to prepare |
| NOUN | analysis | [2] | record | [4] | process | [6] |

3 Now match each verb–noun pair in the table to the correct expressions below, as in the example.

to do a complete   [1] *analysis* —[2] *analyse*   the reasons for our success

to fix a date for   [3] —[4]   the goods on time

to reach a final   [5] —[6]   a name for the new product

to explain the production   [7] —[8]   orders from customers

to do the necessary   [9] —[10]   the production schedule

to keep a detailed   [11] —[12]   the results of the tests

58

1 Listen to these sentences and check your answers to **3**.
2 Listen again and underline the stressed syllable for each verb and noun, as in the example.

5 Read the text below and decide if these statements are true (T) or false (F).

1 The accountant said she was late because the work was difficult. ....
2 The writer accepted the reasons that the accountant gave. ....
3 In a project, there will always be surprise events that take up extra time. ....
4 The accountant didn't know what the writer's deadline was. ....
5 When you're never on time, it's stressful for other people too. ....

JUST DO IT!

Sorry, I didn't have enough time – I had to take the kids to school.

Recently my accountant gave me one of the most common excuses for some work being late: 'It was really complicated and *took me a great deal of time*.' If you think about it, I think you'll agree that this is a ridiculous excuse. All it really does is to ensure that you'll continue to be late, as well as making you feel that you are always *behind schedule*.

Every project takes a certain amount of time. And the truth is that in most cases, you can estimate the time it will take to complete a task. Of course, there will always be unpredictable factors, but in your scheduling you can allow time for these unknown elements.
For example, my accountant knew very well that the work she was doing

for me was quite complex and that she would need to spend a lot of time on it. She also had the advantage of knowing the date on which I had to give my form to the tax authorities *in time* for the deadline. So why did she wait so long to begin? And why did she use the 'really complicated' excuse instead of admitting that she waited too long to get started?
Many of us do the very same thing in our personal lives too. If we always use the 'I didn't have enough time' excuse, we will only continue making the same mistake in the future.
The only solution is to admit that in most cases you do have the time, but you must start a little earlier in order to finish *on time*, or even *ahead of schedule*. So if you're constantly running late, and this is creating stress in your life and stress for other people, you know what to do!

6 Complete these sentences using the expressions in *italics* in the text, as in the example.

1 It ..*took me a great deal of time*.. to find your company because I didn't have a map.
2 Production is .... because we've had two big breakdowns in the factory.
3 The project is less complex than we thought, so we're ....
4 The train left late but arrived exactly ....
5 He arrived at the company just .... for the meeting.

FOCUS ON GRAMMAR: *The passive*

1 The IT manager of a fast-food chain is explaining how the order and delivery process works. Complete the dialogue with these expressions.

this brings me to	once	is packed	the next step
is placed	are processed	after that	first of all
is prepared	are called	are given	is sent

A So what do you do when a customer calls in with an order?

B Well, ¹.......................... the computer checks which restaurant is nearest his home.

A And then?

B After that the order ².......................... automatically via our Intranet to the restaurant.

A So what's ³.......................... ?

B Well, we always have a certain number of dishes ready cooked. If the dish ⁴.......................... in advance, then it ⁵.......................... immediately in a box, ready for delivery. If not, there's usually a five- or ten-minute wait.

A So ⁶.......................... the food is ready, what happens ⁷..........................?

B The delivery addresses for all the orders ⁸.......................... by the computer, which calculates the best delivery routes. Then the delivery drivers ⁹.......................... a computer print-out with a map which shows where they have to go, and in what order.

A That's very efficient. And how does the customer pay?

B There are two possibilities. Either he can pay at the beginning once the order ¹⁰.........................., or he can pay the delivery driver, by card, cash or cheque. And ¹¹.......................... the final stage: after-sales. All new customers ¹².......................... by our customer service department a day later to ask if they were happy with the service. If they aren't, we offer them a free meal.

2 Read the extracts below and on page 61, and put the verbs in brackets into the present passive form, as in the example.

LONDON
09:30

How does email work?

Just as a letter stops at different postal stations along its way, email (send) ¹ *is sent* .... from one computer to another as it travels over the Internet. These computers (call) ².......................... mail servers. Once the messages (send) ³.......................... to the destination mail server, they (store) ⁴.......................... in an electronic mailbox. After this, they (retrieve) ⁵.......................... by the recipient when he opens his mailbox. In many cases, this whole process (complete) ⁶.......................... in just seconds.

retrieve: find

Sending and receiving messages

To send and receive email, two things (need) [7]... :
– An account on a mail server. This is similar to a postal address where letters (receive) [8].. and (keep) [9].................................... for you until you want to collect them.
– A connection to the Internet via a modem. These days, most computers (equip) [10]................................ with a modem, as well as the software which (require) [11].. to access the Internet.
When your mail server account (open) [12].. and your Internet connection (establish) [13].., you are ready to communicate with any other email user, anywhere in the world!

establish: start, set up

3 **1** Read this text about personal organization services. Find verbs in the text to complete the summary below and put them into the present simple passive form, as in the example.

Personal organization services: The National Association of Professional Organizers (NAPO) can provide the name of a Personal Organizer in your area.
Time needed: 1 to 2 hours for initial consultation.

Overview / Example: Julie Morgenstern, an organizer in New York, says once she's finished rearranging your office furniture, she reorganizes your filing systems 'so you can open up a drawer and find what you want in less than 30 seconds'.
Ideas: For filing, Morgenstern

recommends dividing all information into 3 to 5 colour-coded categories (yellow for people, green for finance, etc.), and then dividing these into alphabetically ordered subsections.
Price: Consultants decide their own fees, from $25 to $250 an hour.

The names of personal organizers [1] *are provided* by NAPO. Two hours
[2].. for the initial consultation. With Julie Morgenstern, your
furniture [3].. and your filing system [4]................................... . She
recommends that all information [5].. into colour-coded
categories. Fees [6].. by the consultants themselves.

2 Read the text about the workshop and complete the summary below with these verbs in the correct form (active or passive), as in the example.

depends / is depended	co-writes / is co-written	calls / is called	~~designs / is designed~~
lasts / is lasted	teach / are taught	attend / are attended	

Workshop:
The Covey Leadership Center's 'First Things First' with A. Roger Merrill.

Overview: Designed by A. Roger Merrill, co-author with Stephen R. Covey of *First Things First*, the workshop teaches people how to prioritize projects and objectives.

Time needed: One day, 8:30 a.m. to 4:00 p.m.
Price: $179 to $209, depending on the number in your group.

The workshop [1] *is designed* by A.Roger Merrill, and [2]..
'First Things First'. This is also the title of his book, which [3]..
with Stephen R. Covey. The workshop [4].. one day. People who
[5].. the workshop [6].. how to prioritize projects.
The price [7].. on the number of people in the group.

FOCUS ON EXPRESSIONS: *Managing your workload and saying goodbye*

1 Your boss is speaking to you. Which of the three replies a, b or c, is the best in each case?

1 Where are we on the Lufthansa contract?
 a We're in Munich.　b They'll be ready to sign on Friday.　c Yes, we are there.

2 We must send out the new brochure – a lot of our customers want to know why they haven't received it yet.
 a Yes, I realize we're ahead of schedule.　b Yes, I know we're running out of time.
 c No, they haven't received it yet.

3 I can't get through to the Purchasing Manager – his line's still busy.
 a I'm rather busy at the moment.　b Can you call him?　c Leave it with me.

4 I'm a bit tied up at the moment.
 a Shall I come back later?　b Can I come in?　c I'm pleased to hear that.

5 Can you take care of the factory visit tomorrow morning?
 a Yes, I'll be careful.　b Sure. What time did he arrive?　c Yes, of course, I'll deal with it.

6 Have you had a chance to contact the office supplies people?
 a Yes, I was lucky.　b No, not yet, I'm afraid.　c Yes, of course. I'll take care of it.

2 Decide what to say in these situations, as in the examples.

You're at a meeting. You look at your watch, and it's now 6.30 p.m. Your plane is at 8 p.m.

1 Is that ....*the time*.. ?
2 I really ...*must go*.. .

It's the end of a dinner party at someone's home. It's time for you to leave.
3 It's been ....
4 Thank you for ....

It's the end of a phone call. It's Friday, and you're calling each other again on Monday.
5 Have a ....
6 Speak ....

It's the end of your company's annual conference. Say goodbye to your colleagues.
7 It was .... again.
8 See .... , I hope.

3 Now match these responses a–h to sentences 1–8 in **2**.

a Yes, and you. ....
b You're very welcome. I'm pleased you had a chance to meet my family. ....
c Thanks. You too. Are you doing anything interesting? ....
d Yes it has. I'm glad you enjoyed it. Sorry about the chicken! ....
e Yes. Shall I call you or will you call me? ....
f Gosh, I didn't realize it was so late. ....
g Yes, I hope so too – if I'm still in the job! ....
h That's a pity. Do you need a lift to the airport? ....

((10.2)) **4** A colleague from your Dutch office has just visited your company for the first time.

1 Listen and respond to your colleague.

2 Now listen to a complete version of the conversation and compare your answers.

END-OF-UNIT PUZZLE Read the clues below and complete this crossword.

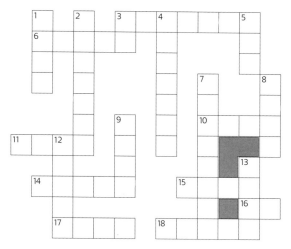

Across

3 Now that we have the results of the tests, we have to .... them.

6 A good time manager always .... his day in advance.

10 The person who receives you in a company is your ....

11 They .... a lot of interruptions at work.

14 I only take a very short coffee .... in the morning.

15 Are you .... that you can deliver to us on the 16th?

16 I'm .... busy that I don't have time to organize my day in advance!

17 You can .... an email to the other side of the world in just seconds.

18 A newspaper editor has to .... the articles that reporters have written.

Down

1 Unwanted advertising by email is called ....

2 Everybody needs to find the right .... between professional and private life.

3 You can change your list of contacts .... often as you want.

4 Our internal email programme only .... messages which come from inside the company – it rejects all the others.

5 You say 'Thank you for inviting me' at the .... of a visit or dinner.

7 If there is a delay on a project, it is behind ....

8 The opposite of early is ....

9 The most boring .... I have to do every day is filling in quality reports.

12 If your computer is attacked by a ...., you can lose all your data.

13 It's a good idea to keep a calendar near your .... so you can see when meetings are coming up.

Tapescript

UNIT 1

1.1

Listen and check your answers. Then listen again and repeat.

1. competition
2. competitor
3. industry
4. manufacture
5. factory
6. employee
7. personnel
8. advertising

1.2

Listen and answer the questions. Then listen again and complete the sentences.

Lands' End, Inc. is a clothing company based in Dodgeville, Wisconsin. It is a mail-order company selling its range through catalogues and the Internet. It has twenty-three sites in the US employing 4,150 people. It employs another thousand staff abroad. Over three quarters of the personnel are female. The company offers an average of 60 hours' training per person annually. With a starting salary of over $21,000 for production staff and over $40,000 for professional people, it is a popular place to work. In 2001 it had over 10,000 applicants for just over one hundred new jobs! Turnover in 2001 was $1,320m. In a market with so much competition, Lands' End, Inc. is doing very well.

1.3

Listen and check your answers. Then listen again and repeat.

1. forty-nine million
2. fifty-eight billion
3. seventeen million, two hundred and ten thousand, eight hundred
4. sixty-six million
5. eighteen seventy-six
6. one thousand, five hundred and two
7. nine hundred and seventy-nine
8. five hundred and forty-three thousand, nine hundred and fifty-five

UNIT 2

2.1

Listen and check your answers. Then listen again and repeat.

1. We are very pleased with this new product.
2. We now want to improve the rest of the range.
3. Our factory can produce 800 units per day.
4. I work for a service company.
5. We are trying to increase our market share.
6. Our design team won an award last year.
7. It is important to research the competition before launching a new product.
8. The advertising campaign lasted two months.

2.2

1 Listen and choose the best answer.

1. Have we met before?
2. Are you new?
3. Your face looks familiar.
4. Pleased to meet you.
5. My name's Peter Jackson.
6. How are you doing?
7. Do you know many people here?
8. How do you do?

2 Now listen and check your answers.

1. Have we met before?
   Yes, we have.
2. Are you new?
   Yes, I am.
3. Your face looks familiar.
   Really?
4. Pleased to meet you.
   And you.
5. My name's Peter Jackson.
   Nice to meet you.
6. How are you doing?
   Fine, and you?
7. Do you know many people here?
   No, I don't.
8. How do you do?
   How do you do?

UNIT 3

3.1

Listen and decide where the passenger is in each conversation.

1

A How many days would you like it for, madam?
B Just two days.
A OK. And do you want to return it to the airport, or leave it at another destination?
B No. I'm coming back here. I have a flight on Tuesday. Is insurance included in the price you gave me?
A Yes, it is madam. But you have to return it with a full tank, or else you pay extra.
B Yes, I realize that, thanks. OK, so where do I sign?
A Just here madam ... and here too. Great. OK, if you'd like to come with me, I'll show you where it is.

2

C It's not working.
B I'm sorry?
C It didn't accept my card. You can try it yourself, but I think it's out of order.

B Is there another one somewhere?

C Yes, there's one just there, but that doesn't seem to work either. It didn't reject my card, but it didn't let me take out any money either. I think it's probably empty.

C OK. Perhaps I'll ask in the bank then. The machines probably belong to them.

B Yes, I think you may be right.

3

D Is it for a special occasion, madam?

B Yes, it's for my sister's birthday.

D How about some earrings? We have a new selection here – arrived just today.

B Mm. Yes, they're very pretty. But she doesn't really wear silver. Have you got any like this in gold?

D I'll see what we've got behind the counter. Can you wait just a couple of minutes?

B Well, not really – they called my plane ten minutes ago. I'll just take this necklace.

D Very good, madam. How would you like to pay?

3.2

1 Listen and respond.

A Hello, my name's Hélène Bayart. You must be Pat Young.

....

A How do you do? I'm sorry I'm a little late.

....

A Thank you for coming here today. I really appreciate it.

....

A So did you have a good trip?

....

A That's good. And did you find your way here OK this morning?

....

A I'm pleased to hear that. Would you like some coffee?

....

A OK, here you are. So is this your first visit to our company?

....

A Would you like me to show you round before we start?

....

A OK. We'll finish our coffee then go on a quick tour.

....

2 Now listen to a complete version of the conversation and compare your responses.

A Hello, my name's Hélène Bayart. You must be Pat Young.

B Yes, that's right. Pleased to meet you.

A How do you do? I'm sorry I'm a little late.

B Don't worry. I was a little late myself.

A Thank you for coming here today. I really appreciate it.

B You're very welcome. It's a pleasure.

A So did you have a good trip?

B Yes, thanks. It was fine. No problems at all.

A That's good. And did you find your way here OK this morning?

B Yes, thanks. Your instructions were very good.

A I'm pleased to hear that. Would you like some coffee?

B Yes, please. Black, no sugar.

A OK, here you are. So is this your first visit to our company?

B Yes, it is.

A Would you like me to show you round before we start?

B Yes, that would be nice.

A OK. We'll finish our coffee then go on a quick tour.

UNIT 4

4.1

Listen and choose the best suggestion.

1 I'm hungry. Where shall we go for lunch?

2 How are we going to tell customers about the new product?

3 I really don't think I earn enough.

4 I'm fed up with our transport company.

5 I really don't feel very well.

6 I find it really hard talking with Americans on the phone.

7 People should talk to each other more in this office.

8 I'd love to work abroad for a couple of years.

UNIT 5

5.1

Listen and repeat.

These words have two syllables: repeat, centre, complain, loyal, invite, survey, advice, offer.

These words have three syllables: encourage, guarantee, satisfied.

These words have four syllables: satisfaction, professional, personalized.

5.2

Listen and answer these questions. You will hear the correct answer when you hear this sound (*).

1 Which country is bigger – is it Portugal or Spain?
  * It's Spain.

2 In which country do people live the longest – is it Canada, the USA, or Portugal?
  * It's Canada.

3 Which country is further from Mexico – is it Venezuela or Chile?
  * It's Chile.

4 In which country do people drink the most beer – is it Germany, Australia, or Ireland?
  * It's Ireland.

5 Which country has a lower population – is it Thailand or South Korea?
  * It's South Korea.

6 Which country receives the highest number of tourists – is it China, Switzerland, or Turkey?
  * It's China.

7 In which country is the population growing faster – in Afghanistan or in Russia?

   * In Afghanistan.

8 Which country has the most populated city in the world – is it Brazil, Japan, or Mexico?

   * It's Japan, and the city is Tokyo.

UNIT 6

6.1

Listen and answer these questions about your future plans. First listen to an example.

A Where are you going tomorrow evening?
B I'm going to meet a friend for a drink.
C I'll probably eat out in a restaurant.
D Perhaps I'll stay at home and watch TV.

Now answer the questions yourself.

1 Where are you going this evening?
2 Are you going to visit anybody this weekend?
3 When are you going to take your next holiday?
4 Where are you going for your next holiday?
5 When are you going to have your next English lesson?
6 Are you going to attend any meetings next week?
7 What are you going to do after you retire?
8 What are you going to do when you finish this exercise?

6.2

Listen and answer the questions.

1 Phoning the travel agent

   A FlightLine Travel. Good morning.
   B Hello, Tina. This is Estelle from Ataca.
   A Hello, Estelle. Are you phoning about Mr Hathaway's plane tickets?
   B Yes. I still haven't received them.
   A Yes, I'm very sorry about that. I'm afraid you won't have them until next Monday.
   B Well, that's a bit late. He's travelling the following day, on the Tuesday.
   A Yes, I do apologize for the delay. It's our busy summer period, so I'm afraid it takes longer to process all the ticket orders.
   B Well, do you think I could have them for Friday if I come and collect them myself?
   A Yes, I think that'll probably be OK. Why don't you come in at about 5 p.m. on Friday? If there's a problem, I'll give you a call. But I'll do my best.
   B OK, Tina. Thanks a lot.

2 In the car park

   C Excuse me. I've just tried to pay for the car park, but your machine has eaten my parking ticket.

D Oh dear. I'm afraid that's not the first time today. There's obviously a problem with the machine.
C Well, could you open it and find the ticket?
D I'm afraid I can't. I have to wait for the manager to come back from lunch. It'll be about fifteen or twenty minutes.
C Well, I have to go back to work. Can I pay you now and you can open the barrier for me?
D No, I'm sorry. I don't have the key to the barrier. The manager has it.
C Well, that's ridiculous! Well, I'll just to have to walk to my office.
D Shall I give you a call when the manager gets back?
C Yes, I'd like to speak to him!
D OK, I'll just take your phone number. I'm very sorry about all this.
C Yes, so am I.

3 Visiting a company

   E Sorry, you did say that Mrs Godot was in room 215?
   F Yes, that's right. On the second floor.
   E Well, I went to the second floor, and there was nobody in room 215. And nobody knew who Mrs Godot was.
   F Oh, I'm very sorry about that. I'll just check the room number again. It was Mrs Godot, wasn't it? G-O-D-O-T?
   E Yes, that's right.
   F Oh dear, I made a mistake. I do apologize. Mrs Godot's office is room 315, on the third floor.
   E Ah, that's why I couldn't find her!
   F Shall I ask her to come down and fetch you? That'll probably be easier.
   E Yes, that seems like a good idea.
   F OK. Please take a seat and I'll give her a call. Could I have your name, please?
   E Yes, it's Mr Beckett, Sam Beckett.

UNIT 7

7.1

Listen to this description. Are the statements true or false?

ING was the result of a merger in 1990 of two large Dutch banks. Throughout the 1990s it made a number of acquisitions all over the world including Mexico, Poland, USA, Germany, and the UK. It is now in the world's top twenty of financial services firms.

ING invests a lot of time and money in its buildings. The Amsterdam headquarters, for example, has 75,000 visitors per year who come because they are interested in architecture. It is an S-shaped building composed of ten towers ranging in height from three to six storeys. They are connected by walkways on whose walls you can find one million dollars' worth of original art. There are no square or rectangular rooms in the complex and the walls slope to conserve energy. Every employee is within six metres of a window allowing everybody the chance to have natural daylight. The company is currently building a new complex near Schipol Airport and this architectural delight is in the shape of a ship or a large shoe, depending on your point of view.

But why does ING invest so much in its buildings? The chairman says it is to show the outside world that it has a human face despite producing nothing apart from paperwork. A flagship building can send out signals about a company and can help improve that company's image. The same chairman finds time to give chocolate eggs to all his staff at Easter, another example of the human touch. The company likes to retain a culture where colleagues work together and individuals are respected. 'We try to keep small firm values in a large company,' says one employee.

7.2

I'd like to begin by telling you a little about the company. As you probably know, William Wrigley arrived in Chicago in 1891 and started selling soap and baking powder. To encourage his customers he gave them free chewing gum. By 1892 he realized that chewing gum was a more popular product and decided to sell it under his own name. In 1893 he launched Juicy Fruit, which is still one of the world's leading brands. It was an immediate success and sales increased dramatically. Over the next twenty years he added other brands and turnover grew steadily. In 1910 he decided to expand overseas and opened a factory in Canada followed by Australia in 1915. The construction of the Wrigley Building in Chicago was begun in 1920 and it is still one of the most famous buildings in the country. In 1939 they used twins as an advertising idea for the Doublemint brand and this idea continues today with the Williams sisters in Wrigley advertisements. With the Second World War sales to civilians fell because all stock was sold to the US army. Towards the end of the century Wrigley developed into the new economies, opening factories in China in 1991 and Russia in 1999. Sales by 2002 had reached an amazing 2 billion dollars. This chart here shows the world market and you can see that the orange segment shows Wrigley with 50% of this market. This table here shows the average American eats 190 sticks of gum per year. Wrigley certainly is one of America's great success stories.

UNIT 8

8.1

Listen. Are the sentences true or false?

A German businessman who runs a fruit import business in Spain set a record recently by spending £42,000 on a round of drinks. It all began when the man offered the owner of a nightclub in London a drink to celebrate his birthday. Having asked for a glass of champagne, the owner was surprised when the businessman ordered nine bottles of Cristal champagne at £250 per bottle. The man then asked the DJ to turn down the music and offered to buy a drink for everyone in the club. At the time there were about 200 people present.

He made a tour of the club taking the orders and offering bottles of Jack Daniel's at £86.50 each when people asked for a single shot. In all he bought 168 bottles. He completed the orders after three hours and signed eleven separate credit card slips. His total bill for the evening was £42,608.25 including a tip for £4,734.35. At the end of it all the owner offered him a drink – 'A coke, please,' the man replied.

8.2

Listen and complete the sentences.

A So what is the plan for the day?
B It depends on the activities. There are six possible activities.
A If I were you, I'd choose a maximum of three.
B Which ones?
A A long one and two short ones.
B So the treasure hunt and two others. OK.
A If thirty people come, how much will they pay?
B €100 each – so if thirty people come, we'll raise €3,000.
A When are we doing this?
B We've got three possible dates – April, May, or July.
A If we chose July, a lot of people would be on holiday.
B Yes, but we'll clash with the Cup Final if we go for May.
A What about the costs? How much will we spend?
B It depends. If we choose the three cheapest events, it'll cost €28 per person.
A So. How many people are coming?
B We're sure of about thirty.
A And the others?
B There are another forty who will probably come.
A So how much money could we raise for charity?
B If everybody comes, we'll raise €10,000.
A OK. Let's look at the details.

UNIT 9

9.1

billboard
benefits
advertisement
brochures
campaign
features
advertise
samples
consumer
promotional
commercial
sponsorship
target
advertising

9.2

1 Listen and match the responses.

a Well, could we just wait a minute or two? Clara's coming to the meeting too – she's on her way.

b Actually, if you don't mind, perhaps we could go on to the final point first of all. You wanted me to talk about that, and I'm afraid I have to leave early.

c Sorry, I'm not explaining myself very clearly. Let me give you another example.

d Well, I'm sorry, but I think we should discuss it now. It's a very serious problem and we never seem to find time to deal with it.

e Yes, if I've understood correctly – you're going to produce a new list of contacts, and I'm going to write a report on the feedback from our present customers.

f Yes, of course. I said that the sales figures for this year are 13% down on last year.

2 Now listen and check your answers.

a A OK, everybody's here. Can we start?
 B Well, could we just wait a minute or two? Clara's coming to the meeting too – she's on her way.

b A I think we've said enough about that point. Can we move on to the next item on the agenda?
 B Actually, if you don't mind, perhaps we could go on to the final point first of all. You wanted me to talk about that, and I'm afraid I have to leave early.

c A Sorry, I'm not with you. Could you be more specific?
 B Sorry, I'm not explaining myself very clearly. Let me give you another example.

d A That's not really on the agenda for today. Can we come back to that another time?
 B Well, I'm sorry, but I think we should discuss it now. It's a very serious problem and we never seem to find time to deal with it.

e A OK. That's everything for today. Can we sum up what we've agreed?
 B Yes, if I've understood correctly – you're going to produce a new list of contacts, and I'm going to write a report on the feedback from our present customers.

f A Sorry, I didn't catch that. Could you say that again?
 B Yes, of course. I said that the sales figures for this year are 13% down on last year.

UNIT 10

10.1

1 Listen and check your answers.

1 We're going to do a complete analysis of our quality system.
2 It's difficult to analyse the reasons for our success.
3 I'm calling to fix a date for delivery of your next order.
4 They never manage to deliver the goods on time!
5 Do you think they'll reach a final decision this week?

6 We can't decide on a name for the new product.
7 Can you explain the production process to me again?
8 As part of my job I have to process orders from customers.
9 The presentation was bad – I didn't have time to do the necessary preparation.
10 Could you prepare the production schedule today?
11 Do you keep a detailed record of all customer payments?
12 We record the results of the tests in this special book.

2 Listen again and mark the stressed syllable for the words you have written.

10.2

1 Listen and respond.

I really must leave now. I have to be at the airport in half an hour.

....

I'm sorry we didn't have time to have dinner together.

....

Well, thank you very much for inviting me here.

....

It was nice to meet you finally and to put a face to the name.

....

And the visit has been really useful – I've learnt a lot.

....

Next time you must come and see us in Amsterdam.

....

So have a good weekend.

....

And see you some time in Amsterdam.

....

2 Now listen to a complete version of the conversation and compare your answers.

A I really must leave now. I have to be at the airport in half an hour.
B Gosh, is that the time?
A I'm sorry we didn't have time to have dinner together.
B Yes, it's a pity. We'll do it next time.
A Well, thank you very much for inviting me here.
B You're very welcome.
A It was nice to meet you finally and to put a face to the name.
B It was very nice to meet you too.
A And the visit has been really useful – I've learnt a lot.
B I'm very glad you enjoyed it.
A Next time you must come and see us in Amsterdam.
B Yes, I'd really like that.
A So have a good weekend.
B Thanks very much. You too.
A And see you some time in Amsterdam.
B Yes, I look forward to it.

Answer key

01 MAKING CONTACT

Focus on words

1
1. Who
2. What
3. Where
4. How many
5. Does
6. What
7. Who
8. Do

2
1. company
2. head office
3. brands
4. production facilities
5. products
6. employees
7. sales
8. CEO
9. competition
10. advertising

3
2. competitor
3. industry
4. manufacture
5. factory
6. employee
7. personnel
8. advertising

4 1 b   2 c   3 a   4 a   5 b

5
1. based
2. range
3. sites
4. employs
5. personnel
6. training
7. salary, production
8. applicants
9. Turnover
10. competition

Focus extra

1
2. 58,000,000,000 – fifty-eight billion
3. 17,210,800 – seventeen million, two hundred and ten thousand, eight hundred
4. 66,000,000 – sixty-six million
5. 1876 – eighteen seventy-six
6. 1,502 – one thousand, five hundred and two
7. 979 – nine hundred and seventy-nine

8. 543,955 – five hundred and forty-three thousand, nine hundred and fifty-five

Focus on grammar

1
2. works
3. travels
4. spends
5. takes
6. flies
7. lives
8. transports
9. contain
10. have
11. plays
12. goes

2
2. Who does he work for?
3. How long does he spend on board?
4. Where does the ship travel (to)?
5. What does the ship transport?
6. Why doesn't he have a lot of spare time?
7. What does he do (when he's) on leave?

3 2 b   3 a   4 e   5 f   6 c

4
2. He works in Turin but he *lives* in Milan.
3. What sort of books *do* you like?
4. I *speak* Spanish and a little French.
5. She loves white wine but she *doesn't* like red at all.
6. Where *does* he *work*?

5
1. is Jack doing
2. is speaking
3. am preparing
4. do you work (are you working)
5. am working
6. am looking
7. work
8. do you do
9. are you calling
10. am learning
11. are you staying
12. am living

Focus on expressions

1 1 Can / Could I borrow your magazine?
2 Can / Could I have another drink?
3 Can / Could I ask a question?
4 Can / Could I use the Internet?
5 Can / Could you give me a hand?
6 Can / Could you send me a brochure?

2 1 Of course
2 No problem
3 I'm afraid
4 Sorry about that
5 Certainly
6 I'm afraid not

3 2 calling
3 speak
4 afraid
5 through
6 line
7 help
8 message
9 call
10 urgent
11 number
12 mobile

End-of-unit puzzle

Horizontal words: buy, brand, recruit, turnover, employee(s), retailer, operate
Vertical words: company, sales, market, consume(r), product, business

02 SHARING INFORMATION

Focus on words

1 2 launch
3 sell
4 improve
5 develop
6 produce
7 trial
8 advertise

2 1 sell
2 development
3 design
4 promotion
5 launch
6 advertise
7 improve
8 trial

3 2 produce
3 trial
4 concept / design
5 improvement
6 Sales
7 launch
8 advertising

4 1 launch
2 advertising
3 development
4 improved
5 trials
6 design
7 product
8 Sales

5 1 d 2 h 3 e 4 f 5 a 6 g
7 b 8 c

6 2 improve
3 produce
4 service
5 market
6 design
7 research
8 campaign

Focus on grammar

1 2 conceived
3 went
4 took
5 founded
6 grew
7 opened
8 was
9 paid
10 designed
11 won
12 supplied
13 merged
14 continued
15 launched

2 1 (He had the idea) In 1895.
2 They went to the barber's or used a cut-throat razor.
3 It was diamond-shaped.
4 The US army (did).
5 (It launched) Brushless shaving cream.
6 (It sponsored) The baseball World Series.

3 2 Where did he open his first office in Europe?
3 How much did Gillette pay to sponsor the baseball World Series?
4 When did the company design its logo?
5 What did it win in 1917?
6 Why did it merge with a competitor in 1930?

4　1 F　2 T　3 T　4 F　5 T
　　6 F　7 T

5　invented, noticed, watched, tried, switched, pressed, tested, developed, decided, costed, advertised, created, started, talked

Focus on expressions

1　1　Have we met before?
　　2　Are you new?
　　3　Let me introduce you to Sally Dutton.
　　4　Nice to meet you, too.
　　5　Do you know many people here?
　　6　Is this your first day?
　　7　Let me introduce you to some people.
　　8　Pleased to meet you, Roger.

2　1　many
　　2　often
　　3　much
　　4　long
　　5　high
　　6　far

3　a 5　b 4　c 2　d 1　e 6　f 3

4　1　What kind of books do you like?
　　2　What places did you visit?
　　3　What hours do you work?
　　4　What's your favourite dish?
　　5　How many / What countries do you operate in?

End-of-unit puzzle

1 b　2 c　3 a　4 a　5 c
6 a　7 a　8 a

03　VISITING COMPANIES

Focus on words

1　1　have
　　2　sign
　　3　pass
　　4　look
　　5　give
　　6　attend
　　7　do
　　8　meet
　　9　negotiate

2　1 T　2 T　3 F　4 F　5 F　6 T

3　1　local attractions
　　2　dining
　　3　snacks, light refreshments
　　4　lounge
　　5　lobby
　　6　healthy
　　7　well-lit
　　8　amenities, facilities

4　2 a　3 d　4 b　5 c　6 a　7 d
　　8 b

5　b 8　c 6　d 7　e 2
　　f 1　g 3　h 4

Focus on grammar

1　(C) room, phone, bag, office, shop, desk, bank
　　(U) news, traffic, information, cash, space, help, luggage

2　1　a, Is
　　2　much
　　3　Are, any
　　4　many
　　5　some, any
　　6　some, much
　　7　any, an
　　8　some, is
　　9　some, any
　　10　are, any

3　2　It costs 24 zl.
　　3　Yes, there are. In fact, most (of them) accept phone cards.
　　4　It's open six days a week, but closes/shuts early on Saturdays.
　　5　Yes, there are. In fact, there are nine.
　　6　I'm not sure, but if you want more information, you can ask / enquire at the information desk.
　　7　Yes, there is. There's a tourist information centre in the Arrival area.
　　8　Yes, there is. In fact, there are two.
　　9　There's a post office in the Departure area.
　　10　Yes, you are. All the duty-free shops are after passport control.

4　1　Car rental
　　2　Cash machine
　　3　Jewellery store

Focus extra

　　2　twenty past eight
　　3　eight thirty-five
　　4　ten past ten
　　5　twenty to eleven
　　6　half past twelve
　　7　quarter to two
　　8　four fifteen
　　9　four forty-five
　　10　five thirty
　　11　five to seven

Focus on expressions

1
1 Would you like a
2 Would you like me to
3 Would you like to
4 Shall
5 Shall
6 Would you like to

2 2 a 3 f 4 g 5 b 6 d 7 e

3 The order is 2, 7, 5, 11, 8, 4, 12, 6, 9, 3, 10, 1.

4 See the tapescript.

End-of-unit puzzle

2 fasten your seatbelt
3 key card
4 shuttle bus
5 have a look round
6 car park
7 book a flight
8 shake hands
9 check out of your room

04 MAKING DECISIONS

Focus on words

1
1 paid
2 pension
3 retire
4 training
5 insurance
6 mobile
7 flexible
8 leave
9 appraisal
10 salary

2
3 advise
4 application
5 recruit
6 / 7 interviewer / interviewee
8 train
9 trainer
10 employ
11 / 12 employment / employer
13 consult
14 consultant

3 1 T 2 F 3 F 4 F 5 T 6 T

4
2 chance
3 hobby
4 initially

5 enough
6 back-up plan
7 regularly
8 award

Focus on grammar

1
2 He was born in 1955.
3 He's been a pilot since 1988.
4 He worked for an executive airline.
5 He's flown 747s since 1994.
6 Yes, he has.
7 No, he hasn't.
8 It was in the garage for two weeks.

2
2 When did he fly for the first time?
3 Why did he get a job as a steward?
4 Where did he work as an instructor?
5 When did he qualify as a pilot?
6 Where has he flown 747s (to)?
7 How long has he worked for / has he had a job with Air France?
8 Has he had a near miss?

3
1 in
2 for
3 since
4 since
5 for
6 For
7 never
8 in

4
3 How long has Mayumi lived in Nagoya?
4 No, they haven't.
5 In 2000.
6 When did Carla join Pirelli?
7 How long did Peter study Engineering?
8 How long has Carla lived in Turin?

5
2 owned
3 worked
4 spent
5 have always liked
6 has recently invested
7 has won

Focus on expressions

1
1 How about
2 sure
3 shall we
4 We could
5 idea
6 Shall I
7 fine
8 don't we

2 1 c 2 f 3 d 4 g 5 a

6 h   7 b   8 e

3 2 Friday, July 14th
   3 Wednesday July 5th
   4 yesterday
   5 Saturday July 15th
   6 next Monday
   7 last month
   8 Wednesday July 19th

4 The order is 5, 7, 13, 16, 3, 11, 9, 1, 6, 14, 4, 8, 10, 12, 2, 15.

End-of-unit puzzle

   2 short list
   3 curriculum vitae
   4 medical insurance
   5 recruitment agency
   6 annual appraisal
   7 paid holiday
   8 job vacancy
   9 mobile phone
   10 flexible hours
   11 pension plan
   12 training course
   13 human resources
   The word that remains alone is 'personnel'.

05 COMPARING INFORMATION

Focus on words

1 1 encourage
   2 loyalty
   3 repeat
   4 online
   5 conduct
   6 deal
   7 centre
   8 meet

2 1 loyalty
   2 invitation
   3 invited
   4 need
   5 needed
   6 satisfaction
   7 satisfy
   8 personalize
   9 complaint
   10 refund

3 2 complain
   3 invitation
   4 satisfied
   5 loyal
   6 refund
   7 personalize
   8 need

4 1 T   2 F   3 F   4 T
   5 F   6 T   7 F   8 T

5

2 syllables: first syllable stress – <u>cen</u>tre, <u>loy</u>al, <u>sur</u>vey, <u>off</u>er
2 syllables: second syllable stress: com<u>plain</u>, in<u>vite</u>, ad<u>vice</u>
3 syllables: en<u>cour</u>age, guaran<u>tee</u>, <u>sat</u>isfied
4 syllables: satis<u>fac</u>tion, pro<u>fess</u>ional, <u>per</u>sonalized

Focus on grammar

1

smaller – bigger
happier – less happy
longer – shorter
the most difficult – the easiest
safer – more dangerous
the oldest – the youngest
fewer / less – more
nearer – further
the least interesting – the most interesting
the lowest – the highest
the most expensive – the cheapest

The word that is left is *better*. The opposite is *worse*.

2 3 F – more expensive
   4 T
   5 F – fewer cigarettes
   6 F – more popular
   7 T
   8 F – much lower
   9 T
   10 F – less tobacco

3 1 the lowest
   2 the fewest
   3 the cheapest, the most expensive
   4 the best, the worst
   5 the biggest
   6 the healthiest

5 See the tapescript.

Focus extra

1 1 c 2 f 3 e 4 b 5 a 6 d

2 1 (about) two-thirds
2 four-tenths / two-fifths
3 ninety-hundredths / nine-tenths
4 just over half
5 nearly a quarter

Focus on expressions

1 1 Do
2 What
3 That's
4 don't think, should
5 I don't
6 so
a 6 b 3 c 1 d 4 e 5 f 2

2 2 I don't think
3 I agree
4 do you think
5 I feel
6 that's a good point
7 do you feel
8 Don't you think

3 1 Participants
2 Agenda
3 Minutes
4 proposals
5 discussion
6 Action points
7 AOB

End-of-unit puzzle

1 call centre
2 repeat
3 contract
4 popular
5 female
6 loyalty
7 improve
8 registration
9 surfers
10 reliable

06 DEALING WITH PROBLEMS

Focus on words

1 1 process
2 ship
3 deliver
4 delivery
5 orders
6 shipping
7 purchase
8 tracking
9 quotation

2 2 track
3 to progress
4 to ship
5 to pay

3 1 cancel, ship / deliver
2 check, quote
3 enquire about, order
4 speed up, follow
5 ask for, prepare / provide

4 2 d 3 g 4 e 5 a 6 h
7 b 8 f

5 The order is 5a, 7b, 1c, 2d, 4e, 3g, 6h, 8f.

Focus on grammar

1 2 are going to launch
3 am going to start
4 will ask
5 are going to invite
6 will check
7 will try again
8 is going to close

2 2 h – are going to fall
3 d – are going to get
4 e – am going to miss
5 f – aren't going to finish
6 a – am not going to get
7 g – is not going to be
8 c – aren't going to find

3 See the tapescript.

4 2 won't
3 won't
4 will
5 won't
6 will

5 a 3 b 5 c 1 d 6 e 2 f 4

Focus on expressions

1 1 I'm afraid
    2 that's a bit annoying
    3 I'll do what I can
    4 I'm sorry
    5 Shall I call the transporter
    6 that's OK
    7 We'll deal with it
    8 I'm very sorry to hear that
    9 Shall I send you
    10 if you could

2

Dialogue 1

Problem: Estelle hasn't received some plane tickets for Mr Hathaway from the travel agent.
Cause: It's the busy summer period and it takes longer to process ticket orders.
Solution: Estelle will collect the tickets from the travel agent herself on Friday.

Dialogue 2

Problem: Someone can't get car out of the car park.
Cause: The machine at the barrier has 'eaten' the parking ticket; only the manager has the key to the barrier, and he's at lunch.
Solution: The person will walk to work; the manager will call later when he gets back.

Dialogue 3

Problem: Visitor to a company can't find Mrs Godot's office.
Cause: Receptionist gave the visitor the wrong office number.
Solution: Mrs Godot will come and fetch the visitor herself.

3 The order is 9, 3, 4, 10, 6, 12, 7, 1, 5, 8, 2, 11.

End-of-unit puzzle

  1 suppliers
  2 stock
  3 snail
  4 keep
  5 express
  6 enquire
  7 shipment
  8 track, order
  9 reminder
  10 reduce
  11 process

07 PRESENTING INFORMATION

Focus on words

1 1 Public Relations
    2 Accounts
    3 Production
    4 Quality Control
    5 Research & Development
    6 Marketing
    7 Sales
    8 Human Resources
    9 Legal

2 1 divided
    2 in
    3 responsible
    4 report
    5 charge of
    6 staff
    7 for
    8 Head

3 2 accountant
    3 receptionist
    4 secretary
    5 lawyer
    6 driver
    7 trainer
    8 manager

4 1 T 2 T 3 F 4 F
    5 F 6 F 7 F 8 F

5

  1 forty-six percent
  2 three billion
  3 two thousand
  4 two thousand eight hundred

6 1 F 2 F 3 T 4 T
    5 T 6 F 7 F 8 T

Focus on grammar

1 2 Where is their headquarters / Where is the company based?
    3 When did the company launch the Grohe Water Technology brand?
    4 How many production facilities does it have in Germany?
    5 Where does it have production facilities?
    6 Why is it developing / does it want to develop its international markets?
    7 When did the company go private?
    8 How many employees does it have?

2 2 You graduated in Communications, didn't you?
    3 Why did you choose Boeing?
    4 Does it have a good reputation, then?
    5 You work in the Commercial Airplanes Division, don't you?
    6 Which department are you working in?
    7 Is that interesting?

8 You are in the Business Career Foundation Program, aren't you?
9 How does that work?
10 Do you have any contacts with the leadership of Boeing?

3 2 don't you
3 isn't it
4 aren't you
5 don't you
6 can't you
7 isn't she
8 doesn't she

Focus on expressions

1 The order is 8, 1, 3, 7, 5, 9, 6, 10, 2, 4.

2 1 soap
2 Juicy Fruit
3 Canada
4 1920
5 twins
6 US Army
7 China
8 $2 billion
9 190
10 50

3 1 decreased rapidly
2 stabilized
3 rose
4 increased dramatically
5 reached a high
6 increased by 100%

4 1 begin
2 here
3 see
4 look
5 shows
6 slide

End-of-unit puzzle

A = Chairman Peter Sing
B = PA Tony Evans
C = R & D Director Cameron Kirkby
D = HR Director Joe Grand
E = Company lawyer Dick Clarke
F = CFO Malcolm Dillon
G = Sales Director Hilary Maine
H = Production Director Becky Piper
I = Head of IT Nick Silins
J = CEO Priscilla Jarman

08 ENTERTAINING

Focus on words

1 2 bean – not a fruit
3 cut – not a way of cooking
4 salmon – not a type of meat
5 soup – not a dessert
6 plate – not something you drink from
7 asparagus – not a dairy product
8 tea – not an alcoholic drink
9 pineapple – is the only fruit

2 1 sweet
2 simple
3 spicy
4 healthy
5 tasty
6 greasy
7 crunchy
8 filling

3 1 F   2 T   3 F   4 T   5 F

4 1 g   2 f   3 j   4 i   5 e   6 d
7 a   8 b   9 h   10 c

5 1 waitress / chef
2 grape / strawberry
3 chicken / duck
4 red / white
5 cloth / leg
6 ham / cheese
7 lunch / dinner
8 cup / glass
9 cucumber / lettuce
10 fry / grill
11 yogurt / butter
12 service charge

Focus on grammar

1 1 April 7th
2 crossbow shooting = cheapest; sailing = most expensive
3 5 (not including lunch)
4 30
5 €100
6 €10 (buffet) or €20 (hot meal) per person

2 1 b   2 d   3 c   4 a   5 h
6 e   7 g   8 f

3 1 were, I'd choose
2 come, will they pay
3 thirty people come, raise €3,000
4 chose July, would be on holiday
5 we'll clash with, go for May
6 we choose, it'll cost
7 comes, (we)'ll raise
4 2 goes, (I)'ll play

3 didn't have, (I)'d finish
4 doesn't speak, (I)'ll translate
5 worked, (I)'d speak
6 earned, wouldn't have

Focus on expressions

1 2 full / fully-booked
3 reservation
4 order
5 starter
6 main course
7 bill
8 credit card
9 taxi
10 service

2 (possible answers)
1 I have a reservation / a table booked in the name of ...
2 Could we have / Could you bring us the menu, please?
3 What is the dish of the day?
4 What would you like / What are you going to have?
5 Can we order, please?
6 I'm afraid my fish is a little undercooked. / Could you ask the chef to cook this a little more, please?
7 Could you pass the salt, please? (to another person at table)
Could you bring me some salt, please? (to the waiter)
8 Could you bring me / Could I have the bill, please?

3 (possible answers)
2 is keen on reading
3 loves watching football
4 can't stand (doing paperwork)
5 is fond of (going to piano concerts)

End-of-unit puzzle

1 c 2 b 3 c 4 b 5 b 6 a 7 b 8 a 9 b 10 c
11 b 12 c 13 b

09 TAKING PART IN MEETINGS

Focus on words

1 1 campaign
2 advertise
3 advertising
4 billboards
5 target
6 Single
7 slogan
8 feature
9 benefit
10 commercials
The product is ice cream.

2 2 sample
3 leaflet
4 kiosk
5 word
6 sale
7 video
8 sponsor
9 general
10 outdoor
11 banner

3
Oo   brochures, features, samples, target
oO   campaign
Ooo   advertise, sponsorship
oOo   consumer, commercial
Oooo   advertising
oOoo   advertisement, promotional

Focus on grammar

1 1 can
2 must
3 mustn't
4 don't have to
5 are allowed to
6 can't
7 have to
8 must
9 is allowed to
10 don't have to

2 1 do you have to
2 have to
3 Are you allowed
4 can't
5 are allowed
6 can
7 don't have to
8 doesn't have to
9 isn't allowed
10 does he have to
11 has to
12 can he

Focus extra

(possible answers)
2 I really must take some more English lessons.
3 I really must look for a new supplier.
4 I really must buy a present.
5 I really must call the IT Support Department.
6 I really must take a holiday.

Focus on expressions

1 1 for coming
2 with you
3 specific
4 come back

5 didn't
6 move on
7 go

2 2 catch that
3 not with, Could you be
4 the agenda, come back
5 said enough about, go on
6 everything, sum up

3 1 a   2 f   3 c   4 d   5 b   6 e

4 1 fell
2 to
3 by
4 increased
5 slightly
6 rose
7 sharply
8 steadily
9 by
10 sharply
11 dropped
12 rise
13 stand at

End-of-unit puzzle
1 promote
2 launched, slogan
3 marketed
4 campaign

10 MANAGING YOUR TIME
Focus on words
1 2 record
3 progress
4 meeting
5 results
6 time
7 task

2 2 delivery
3 to record
4 decision
5 to process
6 preparation

3 3 delivery
4 to deliver
5 decision
6 to decide on
7 process
8 to process
9 preparation

10 to prepare
11 record
12 to record

4 See stressed syllables in 3 above.

5 1 T   2 F   3 T   4 F   5 T

6 2 behind schedule
3 ahead of schedule
4 on time
5 in time

Focus on grammar
1 1 first of all
2 is sent
3 the next step
4 is prepared
5 is packed
6 once
7 after that
8 are processed
9 are given
10 is placed
11 this brings me to
12 are called

2 2 are called
3 are sent
4 are stored
5 are retrieved
6 is completed
7 are needed
8 are received
9 (are) kept
10 are equipped
11 is required
12 is opened
13 is established

3 Part 1
2 are needed
3 is rearranged
4 is reorganized
5 is divided
6 are decided

Part 2
2 is called
3 is co-written
4 lasts
5 attend
6 are taught
7 depends

Focus on expressions

1 1 b 2 b 3 c 4 a 5 c 6 b

2 (possible answers)

3 a wonderful evening
4 inviting me
5 good weekend
6 to you on Monday
7 great to see you again
8 you again next year

3 a 7 b 4 c 5 d 3 e 6
f 1 g 8 h 2

4 See tapescript.

End-of-unit puzzle

Across

3 analyse
6 plans
10 host
11 have
14 break
15 sure
16 so
17 send
18 check

Down

1 spam
2 balance
3 as
4 accepts
5 end
7 schedule
8 late
9 task
12 virus
13 desk